About This Book

It has become an epidemic in America: The knee-jerk reaction to every instance of violence or mayhem is a cry for more gun control. This is an issue that is rarely split along party lines; underneath it all, it is and always has been THE FREEDOM LOVERS vs THE POWER SEEKERS.

This book will examine the constitutional, historical, and foundational basis of gun control and those leaders who have embraced it. It expresses a practical view of gun ownership and emphasizes the laws and views of those who first wrote the Bill of Rights, which guarantees the right of all law-abiding Americans to keep and bear arms.

The bottom-line issues related to gun control are:
- Does gun control reduce crime and thereby make us safer?
- Does gun control pose any risks to our safety or security?
- Is gun control lawful and constitutional?

When we honestly come to understand the answers to these three questions, we will see how today's *polimagicians* and their distractingly beautiful assistants – the mainstream media – create elaborate performances designed to fool us into giving up the one freedom that will allow all other freedoms to be taken away.

THE
MAGIC
OF
Gun Control

By Sheriff Richard Mack

The Magic of Gun Control

Copyright © 2011 by Richard Mack

First printing, 2011

ISBN-10: 0-9848856-0-9
ISBN-13: 978-0-9848856-0-2

Printed in the United States of America

For additional copies, please visit
www.sheriffmack.com

Edited by Kelly Van Shaar
Cover design, book design & publishing by

www.vanshaar.com

Dedication

To my children and grandchildren, and to yours as
well, and to all those who risked their lives,
fortunes, and sacred honor to create the miracle
known as America, and to all those today who do
the same to keep us free.

In Memory Of

My mother and father, Ruth and Wayne Mack
Dr. W. Cleon Skousen
Radio host Derry Brownfield
Nye County Commissioner Dick Carver
Judge John M. Roll
Civil rights hero Rosa Parks
Vietnam war hero Walter Bruce Foote

All who have died for American Liberty

TABLE OF CONTENTS

If "We The People" of the United States of America are ever disallowed the use of firearms, then our country as it was envisioned and constructed by our Founding Fathers will cease to exist. If our arms go then all goes!

Preface

"They're Gonna Squash Me Like a Pumpkin Seed!"

All I ever wanted was to be Sheriff in my rural southeast Arizona home town of Safford, and raise my family in that peaceful atmosphere. In 1988 I was elected Sheriff of Graham County, Arizona and re-elected for a second term in 1992. I never anticipated suing the Federal Government while serving as a small-town sheriff, but that's exactly what happened.

I remember the Brady Bill being signed into law in November of 1993 by President Clinton. For some symbolic reason, Clinton used 13 pens to sign the Brady Bill. James Brady was in attendance; the legislation was named for him. He was Reagan's press secretary and was shot during the assassination attempt in 1981 of President Reagan. During this signing ceremony, President Clinton expressed one of the most classic of all his political propaganda masterpieces. He said, "The Brady Bill will make the streets of America so safe that our nation's police will not even need to carry guns anymore." (I have often wondered, if cops need guns then why don't citizens? Don't citizens need them for the same exact reasons that cops need them; just in case?) I certainly was not going to sue Clinton over his nonsense; I took it for what it was worth: more Washington, DC entertainment. Not once in his statements, however, did he mention the truth about the Brady Bill's enforcement being conducted by the local sheriff.

On January 21, 1994, I attended an Arizona Sheriffs' Association meeting in Phoenix. Twelve of the fifteen Arizona sheriffs were in attendance, along with three well-dressed strangers. It turned out these three were federal agents of the Bureau of Alcohol, Tobacco, and Firearms (BATF). They were assigned to deliver to each sheriff a twenty-page document which, according to them, contained our "marching orders" as to how we, the sheriffs, were now obligated by the United States Congress to work for them for free! There was no negotiation, no contract, no discussion. We were being dragooned into federal service against our will and if we didn't like it, well, we could be "fined not more than $1,000, imprisoned for not more than 1 year, or both."[1] This is the

---

1 Actual language from the so-called Brady Bill. It can be

first time in American history that Congress promulgated legislation which required a state or county official to comply with an unfunded federal mandate under a threat of arrest!

Of course, it took three agents to disseminate 12 copies of this federal trash; that's government efficiency for you. They exited rather apologetically and the cursing started something fierce. None of the sheriffs supported this ridiculous bill, which required us to do background checks on every citizen who wished to purchase a handgun within our respective jurisdictions. Most sheriffs did not have a problem with background checks but with the arrogance of the Federal Government in thinking they could commandeer sheriffs for federal bidding while threatening to arrest us if we failed to go along.

All of us in the room knew very well that the sheriff does not work for the Federal Government, the US Congress, or the president. If that were the case, the sheriffs of this country would have to call Washington, DC each Monday morning to ask their "bosses" what they should be doing that week. This is why we have local elections. This is why we have government of, for, and by the people rather than government of, for, and by the government. This is the beauty of a constitutional Republic, where the rights of the *people* are paramount. This is acknowledgment of state sovereignty and local

---

found online at http://usgovinfo.about.com/library/ bills/blbradyact.htm

3

autonomy.

However, as the cussing waned and the discussion dragged on, each sheriff was asked his opinion as to what we should do about this federal arrogance and usurpation. Each of the other sheriffs agreed to go along with it. "You can't fight city hall," was the most common theme expressed by these Arizona lawmen. I was the only holdout. I told the rest of the sheriffs that I would never go along. "All of us have stated and we all know that the Federal Government cannot tell us what to do. Then why would we go along with this unlawful piece of Washington, DC crap?" After I said this I was hoping to get at least one "Amen." The room was overcome with silence; the sheriffs just looked at me.

I left very disappointed and discouraged. There was just no way I could go along with this "law." I had a three hour drive home and the entire journey was one of deep reflection and brooding. About half way home I decided two things: 1) I was not going to comply with the Brady Bill, and 2) I was not going to hide from this by quitting my job. However, my brooding continued. I had to find a way to deal with this. What was I going to do?

Then as I approached my home it hit me! "I am going to sue my own government!" I knew this was the only way out. I was scared to death: David taking on Goliath! I knew this was the only alternative, yet I knew this was dangerous, crazy, and probably the end of my career. I could not imagine how I would break this startling news to my wife. When I walked in the house, there she was waiting for me. Being so preoccupied with this decision, I just blurted it out.

"I'm going to sue the Federal Government and it's going to cost us everything and they're gonna squash me like a pumpkin seed!" The pretty little blonde girl just looked at me rather bewildered and asked, "Don't I get a kiss?"

So I obliged, of course, then added in an apologetic tone, "I'm serious. I'm going to sue the Clinton administration over the Brady Bill, and I am sure it will cost us our home and job and career." Now this is when the decision was really made. If she had said anything negative, like "Are you nuts?" (Which would have been a natural response) I would not have done it. She did not remind me about the precarious situation this might put our five children in or how much we sacrificed to get this sheriff job in the first place. No, there was nothing like that whatsoever. She simply said, "I am sure I don't understand what you're talking about, but I understand you. And besides, we weren't really looking for a job when we landed this one." She also commented that perhaps this was the reason I was supposed to be sheriff.

I said simply, "I'll take that as a yes" and she just shrugged and went about her business getting the kids to bed.

Well, the next morning when I went to work I had no idea how to begin. Should I call one of the lawyers downtown and ask him to help me with this lawsuit? "No way," I thought to myself, "He would just say what my wife should have said, 'Are you nuts, Sheriff?' Or he might say what all the other sheriffs already said, 'You can't fight city hall, Sheriff; don't waste your time.'"

I had no place to turn. I was not a member of any group or any national organization that might lend support for such an undertaking. Just then my under-sheriff walked into my office and I remembered that he was an active member of the NRA. So I asked him if the NRA had a phone number that might be available for people to call to get advice. He handed me his card and said, "Here's the number, but I have no idea what you'll get from it."

So, I called the number and got put on hold and passed around and after 15 to 20 minutes of this I had just about given up. Finally, I landed in the office of one Richard Gardiner, an NRA lawyer. I told him who I was and what I wanted to do. His response was like manna from heaven. He said, "Sheriff, we've already been preparing the paperwork on this case and we've been praying that you would call."

I was thrilled! I could not believe my ears. I had made the decision to sue just the day before and now there was a national gun rights organization offering to provide lawyers and money to make it all a reality. In my excitement I said, "So we're going to prove once and for all that the Second Amendment does in fact protect and guarantee a sacred right to keep and bear arms, just as the Founders intended!"

Gardiner immediately put me in my place with, "Calm down Sheriff, we are not even suing over the Second Amendment. In fact, law enforcement officers are all exempt from Brady background checks." I was shocked, but intrigued. I replied incredulously, "OK, you're the NRA; you're the second amendment guys. So what paperwork have you been preparing?" Gardiner assured me that a Tenth Amendment challenge was even more appropriate and that their case was airtight. "The Federal Government has no authority to tell you to do anything," he said with absolute confidence. I replied with, "Even better!"

I also told Gardiner that I wanted my own lawyer on this lawsuit, because I wanted to be sure that this did not become the NRA lawsuit. He assured me that that would be no problem and that they would be happy to work with my lawyer. I then asked if he could recommend an attorney in Arizona who had a fundamental grasp of the Constitution and the Second Amendment. Gardiner mentioned Dave Hardy from Tucson, a former NRA lawyer, so I called Hardy and retained him as my personal attorney.

Then on February 28, 1994 (the very day the Brady Bill took effect), Hardy – along with the NRA lawyers – filed in Federal District Court in Tucson, Arizona, a lawsuit: Mack v. US. The case was filed in the court of Judge John M. Roll; yes, the Judge who was murdered by a crazed lunatic in Tucson on January 8, 2011. (There is a later chapter dedicated to Judge Roll.)

In spite of the lawyers, I still felt I was all alone; David versus Goliath or perhaps Daniel in the lions' den. A small-town sheriff from Graham County, Arizona, taking on the gargantuan Federal Government. I was nervous, scared, excited and never thought for a moment that we could win this. Then a few weeks later Sheriff Printz from Montana filed the same lawsuit and then Sheriff Koog in Texas, Sheriff McGee in Mississippi, Sheriff Romero in Louisiana, Sheriff Anders in Wyoming and Sheriff Frank from Vermont. Seven. Seven small-town sheriffs standing for what they believed in, risking everything to put the tyrants back where they belong!

Eventually, all seven of us made the same choice to stand and fight the Federal Government to stop the Brady Bill in court. Only seven sheriffs out of more than three thousand telling the feds, "We will not obey." (I don't even want to think what that percentage would be.) Each sheriff won at the District Court level except Sheriff Koog from Texas. (How does a sheriff lose a states' rights/gun rights case in Texas? Heaven only knows, but he did.) However, Printz and I went to the Ninth Circuit Court in San Francisco on appeal from the feds and we got overturned. Of course, the Ninth Circuit is the most liberal and overturned court in America, so we were expecting that. However, Koog and Romero made a huge comeback by winning in the Fifth Circuit Court in New Orleans.

At this point we had two conflicting appellate courts on the same case, which my lawyers said would all but guarantee us a trip to the Supreme Court. Sure enough, on December 4, 1996, Sheriff Printz and I appeared before the nine Justices of the US Supreme Court. Printz and I had been consolidated into one case at the Ninth Circuit and so it was at the Supreme Court. I remember sitting near James Brady and shaking his hand as I introduced myself. He was very friendly and said he admired me for what I had done. He was very gracious; his wife, Sara Brady, well, let's just say she wasn't.

Then on June 27, 1997, the United States Supreme Court, in a 5-4 split decision, ruled that the Brady Bill was indeed unconstitutional, and that the Federal Government could not issue directives to the States or to their political subdivisions. The Federal Government was forbidden to compel the States "to enforce or administer a federal regulatory program.... such commands are fundamentally incompatible with our constitutional system of dual sovereignty."[2]

It was a modern miracle: We had actually won! But no good deed goes unpunished. The entire suit took three and a half years, I lost my third election and suddenly found myself unemployed with no savings and no way to support my family. We ended up having to move back in with my mom. But when I read the monumental ruling by Justice Antonin Scalia, none of the blood, sweat and tears mattered to me. One sentence from his opinion made it all worthwhile:

"But the Constitution protects us from our own best intentions."[3]

Here was one principle that proved the Constitution was still the supreme law of the land. Either the Constitution means what it says or it doesn't mean anything at all!

I had studied the Constitution; I read about the Founding Fathers and what they intended the Constitution to do: **The Constitution would be the chains by which all politicians would be bound.** (Has anybody noticed any "bound" politicians lately?) This is what the Founders meant and this is

2 Justice Scalia, Mack/Printz v. Unites States (95-1478), 521 U.S. 898 (1997)
3 Justice Scalia, Mack/Printz v. Unites States (95-1478), 521 U.S. 898 (1997)

the purpose of the ultimate American law: to *limit* government, keep it checked and balanced, and to guarantee its impotency!

I knew what the Second Amendment said. I knew the intent of the men who wrote it. I was never much of a gun enthusiast and I never hunted in my life, but I knew what liberty was and I knew that the right of 'We, The People' to keep and bear arms was specifically and solely about liberty. As a sheriff and a peace officer, I had sworn an oath to uphold and defend the United States Constitution. I filed this lawsuit merely because I swore an oath and, I actually read the documents I swore to "uphold and defend."[4] It's just that simple; nothing more, nothing less.

We are not facing the destruction of the American dream today because we are following the Constitution too strictly; far from it! The Constitution was and must remain our foundation. If we allow our politicians to ignore or trample or otherwise destroy our foundation, the rest of the American edifice will not survive; collapse is inevitable. We are currently witnessing the collapse. Although this has been occurring for several decades it has accelerated astronomically the last few years. The solution to our demise does not lie ahead of us; it will not be fixed by creating more laws or more government regulations; quite the contrary. It lies behind us. If we return to

---

4   From the oath of office sworn by all duly elected public officials, as required by the Constitution.

11

those basic and fundamental principles of freedom upon which America was born, we will win. If we do not, well, look around for yourself: We are sowing the seeds...

Introduction

THE POLIMAGICIANS

For as long as anybody can remember, magicians have made a living performing for the public. However, these entertainers do not actually perform real magic. They don't create flowers out of thin air, nor somehow pull a live rabbit out of an empty hat. The Great Waldo did not actually cut a woman in half and then put her back in one piece. Houdini did not really make himself disappear and then reappear in a different part of the theater. These were all illusions. Some of the great magicians of our time have become even more sophisticated in their ability to create amazing illusions. David Copperfield is a Las Vegas institution and a master illusionist who convinces audiences that he can make an elephant disappear, or a car, or even an airplane. The audience really wants to believe what they have seen. However, the magician has no magic and can do nothing of the sort. It's all an illusion. It *is* astonishing and entertaining, though. Audiences marvel at feats and ask each other in total bewilderment, "How did he do that?" But the illusionist cannot defy the laws of nature and dissolve cars, airplanes or people and put them back together in a matter of seconds in another location. It's *impossible* and *everyone knows it.*

Similarly, there are numerous leaders and politicians who want the audience (citizens) to believe they are magicians. The magic they are peddling is an illusion; it is propaganda, but they're pretty sure they can get most of us to buy most of it, most of the time. "There's a sucker born every minute,"[5] and nowhere is this more evident than in the magic world of politics. These political magicians (or **Polimagicians** as I'll call them) have been making their livings with such schemes for centuries. Illusions produced by kings, dictators, presidents, prime ministers and emperors have promised change, hope, peace, freedom, the end of poverty, equality, jobs for all, less taxes, fair regulations and better education. The government will feed you, clothe you, take care of you, and of course, provide you with health care. (All free, of course.) There is no magic in these words; *they are all illusions.* History and reality prove they are nothing more. Perhaps the most stark and vivid example of such illusions is

---

5 Tradition attribues this quote to PT Barnum, but it most likely came from a con man rather than a circus master. That fits very well. http://en.wikipedia.org/wiki/There's_a_sucker_born_every_minute

the propaganda of gun control promising to make us all safer, freer, and more secure. Such promises are empty, false, and the ultimate illusion.

Never in history has gun control provided safety, reduced crime, created peace or given security to any person or nation. Nevertheless, the promises keep coming and we hear them louder after every new highly-publicized violent gun crime. One example recent to this publication was the January 8, 2011, shooting in Tucson, AZ which resulted in 19 people being shot, 6 of them fatally. We all agree that this incident was the most unimaginable tragedy and an unspeakable act of lunacy and cowardice. Of course everyone wants to stop such acts or reduce their frequency. Today's *polimagicians* would have us believe we accomplish it through more gun control. They want us to believe that somehow, some way, gun control is *MAGIC* even though we all know – or at least we should know if we've studied history – that gun control is dangerous, enslaving, racist, and a tool for dictators to control the masses. We want to feel safer; we want to believe it, so we do. These wizards know if they wave their political wands just right and say the magic words while their beautiful, scantily-clad assistants (the media) distract us, *we will buy it.*

They convince you that there is magic in calling 9-1-1; that someone *with* a gun will be there in time to save you. They want you to believe there's magic in not having your own gun, that "you'll be safer that way!" They expect you to buy the illusion of disarming yourself for safety, while what you're actually doing is making yourself an easier target for thugs, gangs, murderers and, oh yes... government tyranny.

It's *magic!* If we all give up our guns – don't take them to schools, or bars, or parks, or banks, or churches, or ballgames – then we will all be safer! And for heaven's sake, do not take a gun on a plane! The plane will fall from the sky if citizens carry a gun. If passengers have guns it will turn the airlines into The Wild, Wild West. The *polimagicians* are really saying, "We will all be better off if no one shoots back when lunatics shoot up schools, kill airline pilots and fly their planes into sky-scrapers, shoot people at church, execute college students in Virginia, or shoot co-workers at post offices. It will be worse if you have a gun and try to shoot back. Only the police can do such a thing. They're trained." This type of propaganda is shoved down our throats daily and some of the peasants are actually buying this Washington wizardry.

The tragedy in Tucson is a vivid example of what happens when citizens are not armed. Several on-lookers called 9-1-1, but it took the police about seven minutes to arrive. (Sorry, no magic). The shooting lasted about 35 seconds, and the only reason it ended was because some courageous (but sadly, un-armed) citizens tackled the assailant. Is there something magical here? (When seconds count, the police are only minutes away!) Do you want such lunatics to be assured that we cannot shoot back? Or would you prefer that they fear each of us? Let the message go out loud and clear: we are armed, we are ready, and we *will* shoot back!

"THIS IS A GUN-FREE ZONE." Have such magic words made our schools safer? Have murderers been discouraged by the signs, laws or local ordinances that disallow guns in banks, churches or on college campuses? No. Yet citizens want to believe that it's all real. The laws and signs will stop the shootings! *It's magic!*

Women across America have tried to stop estranged husbands or boyfriends with restraining orders or orders of protection. Those are magic too! Those pieces of paper will actually stop bullets! Some who believed this illusion have suffered horrible deaths at the hands of men they knew were coming. Many of these women died while waiting for permits or background checks or simply because the government said, "You have to wait, because we think it's best if you do."

The MAGIC of gun control is plain and simply this: *There is none!* If you want magic or illusions go to Las Vegas or Disneyland. But if you want freedom and the reality of self-preservation, arm yourselves and protect your families with the best tools and methods available.

There is hardly a shooting tragedy in this country

that an armed citizen could not have stopped. Why must we wait for a cop to do what many of us could do right then? What are unarmed citizens to do while they wait for the police to show up: throw their cell phones at the mad gunman or tackle him? Are you seeing through the illusions? More importantly, are you seeing the illusionists? They are trying to convince you of magic that never has been and never will be. The lies and deception will continue. "Trust it not sir, it will prove a snare to your feet."[6]

---

6 Patrick Henry, March 3, 1775

Chapter 1

MAMA SHOT THEM

In the infamous case of Warren v. District of Columbia, a woman was gang raped for fourteen hours even though she had phoned the police twice before the rapists gained entry into her apartment. The police never responded. Ms. Warren sued the District of Columbia for negligence and for failure to protect her, but the court ruled in favor of the police, stating that the police have no lawful requirement to protect citizens and therefore, cannot be held legally accountable for failing to do so.[7]

There are not enough police to protect DC residents, nor are the police in DC duty-bound to protect their own people. But here's the irony of all ironies: Our nation's capital, which says it can't protect its citizens, also prevents those same citizens from pro-

---

7   Warren v. District of Columbia (reference needed)

tecting themselves, *and* even arrests them if they attempt to do so. This is not magic. This is criminal! Thousands of our politicians are throwing us to the wolves!

Thankfully, another DC resident, Rebecca Griffin, *did* have a gun. Rebecca Griffin was a motherly woman, a devout Christian and a person of peace. She was known throughout the neighborhood as "Mama." In December of 1993 "Mama" used an unregistered firearm to defend her family from certain death.

Mama's daughter was a witness against two gang-bangers in a pending felony trial. The threats of harm towards her family had been obvious and frightening. One day, Mama heard her daughter screaming: The unspeakable was happening. Two thugs were in her daughter's room, tying her up with duct tape and threatening her with knives. Mama knew she had to act quickly and decisively. She had never owned a gun and never wanted to; she had never been trained to use a gun or even shot one. Suddenly, she remembered that her boyfriend, before he passed away, had left his little revolver hidden in her closet. It had completely left her mind until the moment she needed it.

She got the gun and confronted the two cowards inside her daughter's room. She did not want to shoot them. Mama and her daughter were both attacked and received wounds from the thugs' knives.

Fortunately, none of these wounds were life-threatening, but now there were going to be some. She pointed the gun and fired two shots. They both hit her intended target, the thug who had just sliced her arm. The other coward took off running and made it out alive, but his partner was not so lucky. He stumbled outside and fell dead on the front lawn. (It merits particular notice here that even though she was an untrained, peace-loving grandmother, the thugs *did not take the gun away from her and turn it on her! Nor did she accidentally shoot herself or one of her loved ones!*)

Immediately after securing her daughter, Mama went into her bathroom and prayed that the criminal she had just shot would survive the wounds she had inflicted upon him. She did not want to hurt anybody, but she also did not believe in allowing these thugs to hurt her family. These two pieces of excrement came prepared to burn the house down. It was all prevented by a woman with her boyfriend's pistol. She saved her daughter's life, sent one gutless thug to prison and his partner to hell. This time, we did not read about innocent people dying at the hands of worthless, cowardly lunatics, and we certainly did not hear a media outcry for more gun control.

It's just too bad Mama didn't ask permission from the government to have that revolver in her home. According to the kings of DC, having a gun in her home for any reason without their explicit blessing

21

was a felony.

What's the worst thing you can do to a magician? *Reveal his tricks.* So naturally, the DC magicians arrested Rebecca Griffin for illegally possessing a firearm. She was not charged with murder, just for possession of a firearm. For saving the lives of her family she was charged with a felony! Herein lies the $66,000 question: Who committed crimes in this incident? Yes, the thugs who broke into Mama's home with the intent to kill and burn the place down absolutely committed several crimes and received their just rewards. But after that; who broke the law? Did this loving and beautiful grandmother commit a crime? Was she acting recklessly? Was she an anarchistic rebel with no respect for the law?

The DC gun control laws contained **no exceptions** for self-defense! Rebecca Griffin had indeed dis-obeyed some local statutes, or at least her boyfriend had, but *she* did not break the law. Even if she had possessed the gun intentionally, she did not break the law. The real criminals were those who violated the supreme law of the land: those who attempted to destroy personal rights and freedoms guaranteed by the United States Constitution. DC politicians have had the audacity to legislate away the right to self-defense, but that does not mean this God-given right magically disappeared! These lawless politicians swore an oath to preserve, protect, and defend the Constitution, then openly and wittingly trampled it under their feet.

Watch them pull the rabbit out of the hat as they rationalize away the rights of the people. How noble of our civic "leaders" to be so willing to sacrifice the safety of their constituents in order to protect them! The right to self-defense and self-preservation IS NOT A LEGISLATIVE PREROGATIVE! Self-defense is not up for a vote!

So answer these questions: Who was at fault here? Who broke the law? Who defied the rules of common sense and decency? Was it Rebecca Griffin or was it the politicians in Washington, DC? The potential answers are truly *MAGICAL!*

Chapter 2

Seeing Past the Illusions

In early 2011, suspects were arrested in Columbus, New Mexico in connection with an extensive and elaborate gun smuggling operation. Were the dozen arrestees members of the Mexican Mafia or the drug cartels? No, this list included Mayor Eddie Espinoza, Police Chief Angelo Vega, and Trustee Blas Gutierrez, among others. The arrests were the result of an investigation that had been ongoing for over a year. Was it not Hillary Clinton and Mexico's Presidente Calderon who claimed guns were being purchased legally in Arizona and then transported into Mexico? This was their way of shutting down legitimate gun businesses in Arizona, but now we see that it was other government officials doing the gun running.

Not to be outdone by the Columbus, NM "public

servants," the Bureau of Alcohol, Tobacco, Firearms, and Explosives, (BATFE) has been doing its own gun smuggling.

You will remember that the BATF (now the BATFE) was the federal agency responsible for the raid at Waco, Texas back in the spring of 1993. At that time, there was a movement afoot within Congress to abolish the BATF and transfer its limited duties to the FBI. So, the BATF needed a big show to demonstrate to Congress how vital they were to the overall Washington, DC picture. They found the excuse they needed with the conflict at the Branch Davidian compound. That fiasco ultimately resulted in the deaths of four BATF agents and 80 civilians, (including 20 children and 2 pregnant women) but afterward, the BATF was not abolished nor consolidated. Instead it was granted more money and more manpower.

Now in 2011, we have one of the BATFE's own agents blowing a whistle louder than the Mt. St. Helen's eruption, with the potential to bring down the entire Obama Justice Department! Special Agent John Dodson was assigned to the BATF Phoenix office as a senior agent in 2010. His responsibility was to prevent guns from entering Mexico. Instead, he was ordered to allow exactly that. Dodson divulged to CBS News that the very federal "law enforcement" agency he is employed by had a policy which essentially allowed high-powered assault rifles to be transported to the Mexican drug cartels! Agent Dodson was so incensed and outraged by this criminal activity committed by his own employer that he risked his job and career and exposed these ATF crimes publicly. Of course, the BATF's stated purpose of this absurdity was to "track" the weapons and then bust the cartels using them. One small side effect of this "ingenious" plan was the fact that these guns were used in the commission of murders and inter-gang shootings.

Supervisors within the BATFE have denied Dodson's accusations and assured CBS that intentionally walking guns into Mexico has never happened. However, these same federal bosses have refused to turn documents over to Senator Grassley, an Iowa Republican and a ranking member of the United States Senate Judiciary Committee who has asked for the BATF to explain themselves. Grassley has also interviewed other BATF agents who have corroborated Dodson's claims. Senator Grassley has expressed his frustration with the BATF's "stonewalling."

Agent Dodson's response to the BATF's denial was, "I'm boots on the ground in Phoenix, telling you we've been doing it every day since I've been here. Here I am. Tell me I didn't do the things that I did. Tell me you didn't order me to do the things I did. Tell me it didn't happen. Now you have a name on it. You have a face to put with it. Here I am. Someone now, tell me it didn't happen." Dodson proclaimed this to CBS reporter Sharyl Attkisson.

This wonderful Federal Government project was named "Fast and Furious."

One other potential problem is the fact that the BATF did all this with approval from the Justice Department (Eric Holder) and even worse, failed to notify Mexican authorities about the operation. To even consider going outside jurisdictional boundaries with such a high-risk plan without seeking the rightful jurisdiction's approval is at the least problematic and at the most, an egregious violation of international law. (The BATF raided the Davidians for much less than this.)

The "collateral damage" caused by this ridiculous operation is that Dodson and other agents noticed that the more guns the BATF sent to Mexico for their "investigative efforts," the more people were being killed in violence in northern Mexico. One month's total was over 950 victims, all shot dead. Dodson found the correlation more than coincidental.

The most alarming aspect of this BATF insanity is that Border Patrol Agent Brian Terry was killed by a Mexican National who just happened to be using a BATF "Fast and Furious" weapon. To add insult to injury, in a dose of extremely suspicious behavior by our own government, three of the four Mexican Nationals involved in the shooting of Agent Terry were released and sent back to Mexico due to a "lack of evidence." This is transparency in government? If this is the stuff we know, what on earth could they be hiding from us?! Whatever it is we can all rest assured that it is for our own good and benefit. Our government is watching over us! If that doesn't scare the hell out of you, then nothing will!

Dodson extended an apology to Agent Terry's family and added that he knew they were getting very little information about his murder. The one piece of indisputable evidence is that two BATF "Fast and Furious" weapons were recovered at the scene.

When Dodson and some of his co-workers brought their concerns to BATFE supervisors, the response they received was an example of caring and class: "Well, if you're going to make an omelet, you've got to crack some eggs." (The new unofficial BATFE slogan.) This BATFE bungle should be the biggest scandal in America since the assassination of John F. Kennedy. Yes, this is far more criminal than Watergate! Watergate was a burglary committed by Republican operatives into the Democratic headquarters located at the Watergate hotel. No one was hurt, nobody was killed, but the media went after Watergate with unrelenting fervor. With this "Fast and Furious" scandal, FOX news covered it and CBS exposed it and has subsequently backed off. Until very recently, the other major networks have virtually ignored it. Within a few years, most people will probably have forgotten about it.

One might wonder why the media is so pro-Obama on this issue. But more importantly, one might ask why the BATF was running guns into Mexico in the first place. When Congressman Darrell Issa subpoenaed records from the BATF after weeks of stonewalling, he finally received mostly-redacted papers, some blackened out entirely. Why? Because the real purpose of this gun running to Mexico was to create a reason to promote stricter gun control laws here in the United States. It was all a fabricated attempt by the Obama administration to create public outcries for more gun control. The truth about all this had to be blackened out or we might have seen how the trick really works![8]

Do you really trust today's leaders? Can you really trust anything a *polimagician* says while directing your attention elsewhere? If not, then why would you want to do anything that would give him more power or control over your life? Did we really fight a war against oppression only to replace it with another form that is equally as cruel and immoral?

Tony Martin
Norfolk, England

Tony Martin was awakened from a deep sleep by an unexpected noise in the house. Nearly paralyzed with fear, he lay in his bed and heard muffled whispers in the hallway. At least two people had broken into his house and were moving his way. With his heart pumping, he nervously reached down beside his bed and picked up his shotgun. He racked a shell into the chamber, then quietly moved

---

8   GOA Newsletter Vol. XXXI #3, July 29, 2011

toward the door and opened it. In the darkness, he made out two shadows. One was holding something that looked like a crowbar. When the intruder raised it as if preparing to attack, the homeowner raised his shotgun and fired.

The blast knocked both thugs to the floor. One writhed in pain and screamed while the second man crawled to the front door and lunged outside. As Martin picked up the telephone to call the police, he knew he was in dire trouble. In his country, most guns were outlawed years before and the few that were privately owned were so stringently regulated as to make them useless. His gun was never registered. Police arrived and informed him that the second burglar had died. Then they arrested Martin for first degree murder and illegal possession of a firearm.

When he was finally able to speak with his attorney, Martin was informed to not worry: authorities will probably plea the case down to manslaughter. What kind of sentence would he get for manslaughter? "Well, if luck prevails only ten to twelve years," came the answer from his lawyer, as if he were announcing a great opportunity for the poor sap who defended himself.

The next day, this shooting was the lead story in the local newspaper. Somehow, Tony was portrayed as an eccentric vigilante while the two men he shot were represented as choirboys. Their friends and relatives could not find an unkind word to say about them. Buried deep down in the article, authorities acknowledged that both "victims" had been arrested numerous times. But the next day's headline said it all: "Lovable Rogue Son Didn't Deserve to Die." The burglars had been transformed from career criminals into Robin Hood-type pranksters. As the days wore on, the story took wings. The national media picked it up, then the international media ran with it. It got worse for the law-abiding citizen at each passing day. The surviving burglar became a folk hero.

Tony's defense attorney said the surviving crook was preparing to sue, and that he'd probably win. The media published reports that the victim's home had been burglarized several times in the past and that he had been critical of the local police for their lack of effort in apprehending the suspects. After the last break-in, he told his neighbor that he would be prepared for the next time. The District Attorney used this information to allege that he was lying in wait to ambush the poor unsuspecting burglars. A few months later the case went to trial. The charges were not reduced, as the lawyer had so confidently predicted.

As the victim (now the accused) took the stand, his anger at the injustice of it all worked against him. Prosecutors painted a picture of him as a mean, vengeful man. It did not take long for the jury to re-turn a verdict of guilty on all charges. The judge sentenced him to life in prison; *life in prison!*

As absurd and unjust as it might be, this case really happened. On August 22, 1999, Tony Martin of Emneth, Norfolk, England, killed one burglar and wounded a second. In April of 2000 he was convicted and is now serving a life term.

How did it become a crime to defend one's own life and property in the once great British Empire? It started with the Pistols Act of 1903. This seemingly reasonable law forbade selling pistols to minors or felons and established that handgun sales were to be made only to those who had a license. The Firearms Act of 1920 expanded licensing to include not only handguns, but all firearms except shotguns. Later laws passed in 1953 and 1967 outlawed the carrying of any weapon by private citizens and mandated the registration of all shotguns. Similar incremental laws have been legislated in the USA.

Momentum for total handgun confiscation began in earnest after the Hungerford mass shooting in 1987. Michael Ryan, a mentally disturbed man with a Kalashnikov rifle, walked down the streets shooting everyone he saw. When the smoke cleared, 17 people were dead. (This is impossible! Indiscriminately shooting people with a rifle is against the law in England! There must have been a mistake. Gun control laws prevent such gun violence. Wasn't Michael Ryan informed about the law?)

The British public, already jaded by eighty years of "gun control", demanded even tougher restrictions. The legislators set their sights on the seizure of all privately owned handguns (even though Ryan had used a rifle in this crime).

Nine years later in Dunblane, Scotland, Thomas Hamilton used a semi-automatic weapon to murder 16 children and a teacher at a public school. For many years the media had portrayed all gun owners as mentally unstable or even worse, criminals. Now the press had a real kook with which to beat up law-abiding gun owners. Day after day, week after week, the media gave up all pretense of objectivity and demanded a total ban on all handguns. The Dunblane inquiry, a few months later, sealed the fate of the few sidearms still owned by private citizens. But again, no handgun was used in the crime that sparked the whole affair.

> *"Laws that forbid the carrying of arms disarm only those who are neither inclined nor determined to commit crimes. Such laws make things worse for the assaulted and better for the assailaints."*
>
> **~ Thomas Jefferson**

During the years in which the British government incrementally took away most gun rights, the notion that a citizen had the right to armed self-defense came to be seen as vigilantism. Authorities refused to grant gun licenses to people who were threatened, claiming that self-defense was no longer considered a reason to own a gun. Citizens who shot burglars or robbers or rapists were charged while the real criminals were released. (So much for the rights of women; doesn't England have N.O.W.?)

After the Martin shooting, a police spokesman was quoted as saying, "We cannot have people taking the law into their own hands." All of Martin's neighbors had been robbed numerous times, and several elderly people were severely injured in beatings by juvenile delinquents who had no fear of any possible consequences. Martin himself – who was a collector of antiques – had seen most of his collection trashed or stolen by burglars. When "self-defense" becomes "taking the law into our own hands" – or in other words, becomes illegal – then we are all doomed to be criminals sooner or later.

When the Dunblane Inquiry ended, citizens who owned handguns were given three months to turn them over to local authorities. Being good British subjects, most people obeyed the law. The few who didn't were visited by police and threatened with ten year prison sentences if they refused to comply. (Of course, such laws were for their own good and the good of society!)

Police later bragged that they'd taken nearly 200,000 handguns from private citizens. How did the authorities know who had handguns? The guns had been registered and licensed; kind of like cars.

Sound familiar? Throughout history, where gun registration has been required by law it has always been followed by confiscation. *Always!*

Maybe it's time we learned that gun control has never provided peace, safety, or freedom. Americans have a guarantee in the supreme law of the land that their gun rights shall not be *infringed*. Which laws should we follow? Which system do you want? Which structure do you trust? Should we try the failed gun control laws of Britain and other European nations or follow the admonitions of our Founding Fathers? When are we ever going to stop believing the *polimagicians*? Do we side with "Big Brother" government or with freedom, personal accountability, and the God-given right to self-preservation?

Tony Martin was a victim. His case is a typical example of the consequences of gun control. Tony Martin, a good man and a law-abiding citizen, went to prison for life as a direct result of gun control. He was victimized by his own government! Did gun control protect him? Did gun control provide peace and security for him and his family? Ah, your answer is magical! You say this was England and such could never happen in America. It already has!

Katrina-style gun control

"It can't happen here." We hear that all the time. The

truth is it *does* happen here and has for decades. A recent terrifying example of government taking care of us was the Hurricane Katrina disaster in New Orleans. FEMA's (the Federal Emergency Management Administration) response is well documented.

When Katrina hit the Louisiana coast, the State and the Federal Government were ill-prepared. Looting and chaos ensued. Evacuations and rescues were sporadic and disorganized. Finally, the Federal Government decided that it ought to do something to appear as if it knew what it was doing. So of course, it decided to confiscate all privately owned firearms. That's right; when chaos and looting and anarchy abound, when the people need their guns for self-protection the most, "Big Brother" stepped in to confiscate guns from law-abiding citizens. I think "Big Brother" calls this the "Second Amendment Hurricane Exception Clause." Why? Because government said so and they're here to take care of you.

When an elderly woman refused to give up her weapon to the "federal servants" trying to "help" her, well, they had to rough her up a little to make sure she got the message! Yes, this was in America! Yes, George W. Bush was president! But he said he supported the Second Amendment, didn't he? The old lady must not have read the exception clause. The print is really small... so tiny, in fact, that no one has ever seen it.   But surely it must be there... somewhere...

> *Never, under any circumstance, ask the government to take care of you. Because they will!*

So how do we prevent the abuse and overzealous actions of our own government? We must first recognize the existence of such threats and take action to avoid similar situations in the future. Do local sheriffs and police actually believe that they must allow, tolerate or go along with the confiscation of guns from law-abiding citizens? Do local authorities have some magical obligation to go along with federal officials who are clearly violating principles of freedom? Is there anything your sheriff or other local leaders could do that would be more important than protecting your rights or your liberty? No, nothing is more important! This is our duty and utmost responsibility and we can and must do it. Yes we can! Yes we can!

The solution is to take care of ourselves. Local communities can make necessary preparations and take preventative measures to provide for the needs of local citizens in the case of most disasters. Why would we ask Washington, DC to be responsible for such emergencies? How can we throw money into the DC cesspool like coins in a wishing well and expect that we will *magically* be saved? If we utilized our own ingenuity and sense of community and retained our tax dollars within our own neighborhoods, we would have money to spare.

After all, we would not be funding private jet flights, expensive parties, corporate bailouts, campaign buses, failed "initiatives" or hundreds of other excesses.

In the Mack/Printz ruling previously cited, Justice Scalia clarified the Federal Government's impotency: "State Legislatures are not subject to federal direction." This also includes county and city legislatures. Scalia opined, "The Federal Government may neither issue directives requiring the States to address particular problems, nor command the States' officers, or those of their *political subdivisions*, to enforce or administer a federal regulatory program.... Such commands are fundamentally incompatible with our constitutional system of dual sovereignty."

The Bill of Rights and this monumental ruling make it more than clear that the Federal Government cannot tell us what to do. To intimate such is to pretend that the Framers – who had so recently risked their lives and fortunes to fight against the all-powerful King of England – did so just to establish another government just as oppressive here in America! As Benjamin Martin (Mel Gibson) described it in THE PATRIOT, "Trade one tyrant three thousand miles away for three thousand tyrants one mile away." The intent of the Founders was to prevent any such recurrences!

"A healthy balance of power between the States and

the Federal Government, will reduce the risk of tyranny and abuse from either front," Justice Scalia said in the Supreme Court case. Maintaining this balance is what he termed, *"One of our Constitution's structural protections of liberty."* State sovereignty then, is a "structural protection of liberty." The question is, who will enforce States' rights and sovereignty? Maybe Obama will appoint a state sovereignty czar? No my good friends. Protecting and preserving State autonomy is *our* responsibility and that of our governors, our state legislatures, our county commissions, our city councils, even our school boards. Freedom is our duty and *nothing* supersedes freedom – not politics, policies, programs, or regulations. When government becomes despotic, we stand in the way; we interpose ourselves for America, one county at a time. And why do we do this? FREEDOM!

Chapter 3

CSPOA HALL OF HONOR

The CSPOA – or Constitutional Sheriffs and Peace Officers Association – is a voluntary association of peace-loving, freedom-loving patriots, sheriffs, and peace officers who stand together to encourage and support our local officials in the fight against tyranny, decay and corruption from within. We seek to educate our local officials on their rights, duties and oaths of office, and to re-establish our country as the Constitutional Republic it was originally intended to be.

This chapter contains accounts from the lives of sheriffs and other public officials who had the courage to keep their word and their oaths of office to uphold, defend, preserve, and protect the United States Constitution. These all men who have stood against tyranny and the corrupt establishment.

Sheriff Jim Alderden
Larimer County, Colorado

On February 22, 2010, the Colorado State Board of Governors voted unanimously to prohibit any students from carrying guns of any kind on both CSU campuses, even if the students possessed a valid permit for doing so. In other words, the CSU Board of Governors was making something illegal that had already been made lawful by the State Legislature. The University of Utah had attempted to do the same thing on their campus just a few years ago. However, their efforts were *shot down* by the State Supreme Court, which said a public university could not make something illegal that was previously allowed by state legislation. So Sheriff Jim Alderden told the CSU Board that he would not allow any students arrested for this farcical regulation to be booked in to his jail! The chief law enforcement authority for Larimer County told the Board of Governors, "Oh no you don't!" The sheriff, outraged by the Board's attempt to put students in harm's way, announced publicly that he would do all in his power to undermine the CSU ban. Sheriff Alderden said he would also go to court and testify on behalf of any student charged with carrying a concealed weapon on CSU campuses. "There are volumes of statistical and anecdotal data that show populations are safer when law-abiding citizens are permitted to carry concealed weapons," Sheriff Alderden stated.

This good sheriff was simply doing his job! He stood

against politicians, he stood against a stupid law, and he even stood against the CSU Chief of Police who supported the gun ban! The sheriff stood with the people, *kept his oath,* and showed the entire country the solution! When government becomes destructive of its own principles of liberty, it takes a little courage from local public servants to protect the people from such criminal behavior. Sheriff Jim Alderden put himself in the way; he interposed himself on behalf of the people. He protected and defended their constitutional rights! For his integrity and courage and for doing his job as required by his oath of office, Sheriff Alderden is hereby inducted into the CSPOA Hall of Honor!

Sheriff Tom Dart
Cook County, Illinois (Chicago)

Sheriff Dart is the CLEO of the second largest sheriff's office in the USA, after Los Angeles. Sheriff Dart had the gall and the jurisdictional authority to challenge some of the biggest banks in the world by informing them (and the courts) that he would no longer perform foreclosure evictions within the boundaries of Cook county. What? A sheriff can't do that! He has no right to stop the banks from "legally" taking homes away from citizens! He can, he did, and yes, it is his job to protect his constituents from injustice.

Sheriff Dart said, "This is so outrageous and these

poor families are being put through this day in and day out by people that don't do their jobs."

"It's so hard for me to stomach these [Bankster] people," Sheriff Dart said as he singled out Bank of America, JP Morgan Chase, and GMAC/Ally Financial. Chase refused to comment about the Sheriff's actions and the other two asked him to be nicer and assured the Sheriff that their paperwork for the foreclosures they had sent him were accurate and legal.

Nevertheless, this county sheriff saw an injustice and interposed himself on behalf of the people he served. He followed through on his promises and ordered his deputies to stop serving the foreclosures. Did the judges try to hold Sheriff Dart in contempt? Did the banks try to sue him? Was Dart charged with a crime, perhaps for interfering with a legal proceeding? No, none of this happened. The banks threw their Popsicles®[9] in the dirt and went home crying, and Sheriff Dart was re-elected in a landslide.

---

9   From http://www.popsicle.com: "POPSICLE® is a registered trademark of Unilever and is NOT a name for just any frozen pop on a stick..." However, the bankers in this example threw – hypothetically speaking – their actual Popsicle® brand freezer pops in the dirt.

Corporal Steve Armbruster – Kutztown, Pennsylvania

Steve Armbruster is a peace officer and corporal for the Pennsylvania State System of Higher Education. There are 300 such officers in Pennsylvania, assigned to provide police services at college campuses across the state. Corporal Armbruster is employed at Kutztown University in Kutztown, PA. In 2007, a street Minister by the name of Michael Marcavage came to Kutztown to preach at the University. Some local officials got their undies all tangled about it and tried to stop the peaceful, open-air preaching by this "dangerous" minister. Marcavage didn't really care who disapproved of him being at the school. He and a group of about 15 people came to the campus to do what they believed they had been called to do: preach the gospel.

The president of the university ordered Officer Armbruster to arrest Marcavage for being on the campus without a permit. Armbruster refused, partly because he knew there was no crime being committed and partly because the university president was not his supervisor. The president called the university chief of police to the scene and ordered HIM to order Armbruster to arrest Pastor Marcavage. The chief of police did so, but Armbruster refused again. He tried to reason with the chief and explained that the preacher was not breaking any laws. The indignant chief relieved Armbruster of his duties and ordered him to leave the area. This order was obeyed as Officer Armbruster saw no alternative.

The chief then ordered other officers to perform the arrests that Armbruster had refused to do. Marcavage, a student from the university and another preacher (Jim Deferio from NY) were all handcuffed and hauled to jail. They were charged with something that should never have been on the books in the first place: the crime of "disorderly conduct." (Cops needed a catch-all violation for people they just don't like or who might offend them at times, so legislatures granted them this excuse. This charge is overused and abused as much as speeding charges from radar tickets.) So what had these three "criminals" done? Basically, in their own way they had refused to get to the back of the bus (see the Rosa Parks chapter). They held signs about repentance and read from the Bible! Yes, some people were offended by this public display of religious activism. Thank goodness we have cops that will stop this sort of thing! Maybe someday we'll have police who keep their oaths and actually defend the rights of the people to free religious expression and the right to peaceably assemble. Maybe we should add these two principles to the Bill of Rights. Then perhaps our governmental officials would uphold and defend such ideals.

So what happened to Officer Armbruster for disobeying his supervisor? Of course, they tried to have him fired. When his chief saw that might not be possible, he decided to suspend Armbruster without pay for five days. Armbruster appealed the disciplinary action and won. He later testified in court for the two preachers. All charges were dismissed against them, and later the same was done for the student who had been arrested with them. This ended with justice being served and Corporal Steve Armbruster being vindicated; however, the arrests of these three innocent citizens should have never happened. "Public servants" with badges and uniforms caused this injustice, while only one did his best to stop it. How do we save America? One Steve Armbruster at a time.

Sheriff Dave Mattis
Big Horn County, Wyoming

Dave Mattis served as sheriff during the 1990s. Sheriff Mattis told the IRS they could not confiscate records from the county recorder's office. He stood in that office and ordered the IRS to get out. They did. But they had their little feelings hurt, so they asked a judge to tell Sheriff Mattis to be more user-friendly. The judge sided with "Big Brother" and told Mattis to allow the IRS to "do their job." The bottom line here is simple; we had a courageous sheriff and a wimpy judge.

Later, Sheriff Mattis was part of a lawsuit regarding an incident that occurred before he took office. It seemed that the INS (Immigration & Naturalization

Service. It's somewhat difficult to keep all these DC agencies straight, isn't it?) came into Big Horn county and asked the sheriff's office to help them serve warrants on the Castaneda family for being in the US illegally. Well, several federal agents and two deputies raided the Castaneda home at 1 o'clock in the morning. The Castanedas were all asleep and terrified by the SWAT style entry into their home. There was just one other tiny little problem with this police action; the Castanedas were all American citizens. The Big Horn deputies went along assuming the INS agents had done their homework. Big mistake. They got sued along with the INS.

In court the Castanedas said they would take the plea bargain as offered by the government with one proviso. They required that the county sheriff develop a policy which would forever prevent such raids and mistakes. So, Sheriff Mattis developed a policy which required all federal agents, regardless of which agency they might work for, to check with the sheriff before they could serve papers, make arrests, confiscate property, or otherwise do anything in Big Horn County. This policy was accepted by all those involved in this plea deal and was subsequently enforced by Sheriff Mattis. Do you think Sheriff Mattis ever took advantage of this authority to tell the feds they could not play in his county? Yes he did, and all sheriffs should do the same. Why? Because that is precisely how we "serve and protect" the people for whom we work. It's not rebellion or lawlessness; it's called a "check and balance."

Sheriff Glenn Palmer
Grant County, Oregon

Approximately 500 of Sheriff Palmer's constituents gathered with him on June 14, 2011, in the Union High School Gymnasium to support him and thank him for keeping his oath of office! You see, he actually believes that protecting the people from the enforcement of stupid laws and out of control government officials is *his* responsibility. So much so that he has put himself on the line and subjected himself to the scrutiny and ridicule of the mainstream establishment as he courageously stood against the US Forest Service. Yes, Grant County, Oregon, a small county of not even 7,000 people and 5,000 square miles, has set the example for the entire country as to how we restore freedom in America! A sheriff doing his job, keeping his oath and standing for liberty with the support of the people.

This did not happen overnight. These people have long endured abusive regulations by the Forest Service. The sheriff has been working for years to have the USFS curtail their whimsical enforcement. The USFS was actually charging and citing people for merely gathering dead wood to use in their fireplaces. Lately, Palmer's complaints have fallen on deaf ears, so he has been forced to take stronger action. Recently, he wrote the Forest Service a letter.

Here it is in its entirety:

Teresa Raaf, Supervisor
Malheur National Forest
Patterson Bridge Road
John Day, Oregon 97845

Ms. Raaf,   March 31, 2011

Regarding the pending cooperative policing agreement between the US Forest Service and the Grant County Sheriff, I am advising you in writing that I will not be signing the agreement. I do not believe that it is in the best interest of the people I serve or the Grant County Sheriff's Office to continue with the agreement.

There are several issues that I will bring to your attention that at this point I will not go into detail about.

The issues include, but are not limited to, how US Forest Service LEO's treated citizens of this county in October and November of 2010, Travel Management Plan, illegal road closures, grazing, logging, wood permits, prescribed burns, unemployment and other socioeconomic issues this community faces today. There is a general mistrust of the Federal Government by the people of this County, State and Nation.

You are aware that I had sent at least two requests to the US Forest Service asking for information that pertains to where the US Forest Service gets its Constitutional authority to have law enforcement officers within Grant County.

One response that I have received in writing is that their authority is given through the Cooperative Policing Agreement that this agency has signed in the past. Upon asking for clarification and a second request, the response was that I needed to check with my District Attorney. Neither response in my opinion is adequate.

49

Under Article 1 Section 8 of the United States Constitution, the Federal Government is limited in its powers and authority. Your jurisdiction as I see it is limited in nature to the Federal Building in John Day.

Within the confines of Grant County, Oregon, the duties and responsibility of law enforcement will rest with the County Sheriff and his designees.

Sincerely,

Glenn E. Palmer
Sheriff for Grant County

So, here we have a small-town sheriff standing against the Federal Government on behalf of his citizens. You know that when this sheriff promised in solemn oath to protect and defend these people, he meant it. He takes his oath seriously and intends to keep his word. He has been ridiculed and sharply assailed for his stance, even by the local newspaper. Others who have been part of this criticism – such as local officials who would never have the courage to do such a thing – certainly have the courage to complain about Palmer. One such coward actually criticized the sheriff, not because he was wrong, but because his stance could cost the county federal funds! In other words, this official is saying Sheriff Palmer should not stand for what's right or try to keep his oath; He should become a political prostitute and grab the federal money! Is this not the political correctness of the day? Don't do whatever it takes to keep your oath of office, do whatever it takes to bring in the money! Thank goodness there are those with the honor and integrity to stay out of the corrupt mainstream. Are we among them?

Again, the fantastic part of this situation is that the people have taken it upon themselves to stand with their sheriff. They even bought an entire page of ad space in the local newspaper, The Blue Mountain Eagle, to get their point across. In the June 1, 2011, issue they published a list with the full names of approximately 600 citizens of Grant County under the headline: **SUPPORT OUR SHERIFF**. The subtitle reads: *The following citizens stand behind our County Sheriff Glenn Palmer, his oath of office and the constitutions.*

This is an example to all Americans, to all leaders of this great country. A small county in eastern Oregon just demonstrated how we preserve our constitutional republic: We have sheriffs who keep their oaths, who stand for liberty, and then we have **the people**. Yes, just as the entire Constitution starts; *We the People* stand with our sheriff!

This is the answer; this is the solution. Grant County and Sheriff Palmer have shown us the way! As sheriffs and other local leaders stand for freedom, we take America back county by county and state by state!

County Commissioner Dick Carver
Nye County, Nevada

While Dick Carver was commissioner of Nye County, he told the feds to get out of his way in 1994 as he climbed aboard his bulldozer and reopened an unpaved rural road that was washed out during a rainstorm. You see, the USFS claimed the road was on Forest Service property. Dick Carver told them the road was in Nye County and had been in continuous use by citizens of the county for the last hundred years. The people who could no longer use the road were mad and frustrated about federal inaction and red tape. They just needed the road repaired. It only needed about two hours worth of work, but the feds told all concerned that the road could not be repaired until environmental studies and a cost analysis were completed. The county did not care about the costs and said they would take care of it, but the feds would have none of this common sense!

After months of public complaints, meetings and attempted negotiations, the Nye County Commissioners voted unanimously to have one of their own, Dick Carver, take his bulldozer to the road in question and fix the damn thing! So Carver and about 150 citizens – some of them exercising their second amendment rights – went to the road and cheered as Carver climbed onto his bulldozer. Two USFS officers stood in front of the bulldozer and ordered Carver to cease and desist. So, Carver turned off the engine, climbed down, and went over to two county deputies who were there to keep the peace. The commissioner said boldly, "Deputies, if these two Forest Service officers put themselves in front of my bulldozer again, I will expect you to arrest them immediately and take them to the county hotel!" The deputies nodded, the USFS agents moved out of the way, and Dick Carver repaired the road.

It bears noting here that no one or nothing was harmed in this incident, not even any trees or squirrels. The road was fixed quickly by the county's regular crew with no extra costs and all concerned went home safely. Nobody went to jail and nobody paid any fines. And what happened to Dick Carver? Well, he was re-elected in a landslide and a few months later was featured on the front cover of TIME magazine. Dick Carver died of a brain tumor in 2002. His life was one of courage and dedication to the Constitution of the United States.

Do you see the equation here? There is no magical formula; just simple math:

One constitutional county sheriff
Plus one constitutional county commissioner
Equals
LOTS of freedom and protection from tyranny

Joe Banister
Internal Revenue Service Detective

All Joe ever wanted was to be an agent for the IRS. He hired on with them in 1993, hoping to go after tax cheats and criminals. Joe Banister is a humble man, soft-spoken, religious, and a dedicated family man. He was not part of some subversive political movement to expose the corruption of the IRS or the Federal Government in any way; quite the contrary. He wanted a career as an IRS agent; that's it.

After several years of service to the IRS, he made a big mistake. He listened. He had heard some of the complaints that citizens had leveled against the IRS: It was making some egregious errors against innocent Americans. Furthermore, Agent Banister received information that a freedom group in California was offering a huge reward if anyone in the USA could prove there was actually a law requiring a citizen to pay an income tax. Joe was sure this was a bunch of nonsense, but decided to investigate it for himself. He figured that such obvious misconceptions would be easy to reconcile. He was wrong. For the next year, all on his own time, Agent Joe Banister investigated the claims made about the IRS and – wouldn't you know it – he could not disprove the claims. So, he took his concerns to his supervisors and handed them a letter detailing his findings. He asked his superiors to set him straight so that he could get back to work. He actually believed they could help him straighten this whole thing out. Banister was wrong again!

Here is his complete letter:

February 8, 1999
Mr. XXXXXXXXXX

Internal Revenue Service,
Criminal Investigation Division
55 South Market Street, Suite 815
San Jose, California 95113

Dear XXXXXX:

This is undoubtedly the most difficult letter I have ever
written in my life. Still, my duty as a citizen, my duty
as a federal law enforcement officer sworn to support
and defend the Constitution of the United States, and
my adherence to the Old Testament's 9th Command-
ment which prohibits me from bearing false witness
against my neighbor requires that it be written. As you
know, I have been employed as a Special Agent for the
U.S. Department of the Treasury, Internal Revenue
Service, Criminal Investigation Division, since 1993. My
education, training, and experience gained prior to being appointed as an agent with the U.S. Department of
the Treasury includes:

- Bachelor of Science Degree, Business
  Administration, Concentration in Accounting. San
  Jose State University, 1986
- 3 years with *KPMG Peat Marwick* as a senior tax
  specialist and staff auditor
- 4-5 years as Accounting and Tax professional in
  private industry and later as a self-employed
  Certified Public Accountant (California license CPA
  57875).

In 1993, my dream of becoming a federal law enforcement officer became a reality when the IRS Criminal Investigation Division appointed me to the position of GS-1811 Criminal Investigator, more commonly known as *special agent*. My duties as an IRS Special Agent include investigating violations of the U.S. Code, specifically the Internal Revenue Code (Title 26), money laundering and conspiracy violations under the Criminal Code (Title 18), and violations of the reporting requirements of the Bank Secrecy Act (Title 31). I am also authorized to execute or serve search warrants and arrest warrants, to make arrests without warrant, to carry firearms, and seize property subject to forfeiture. In addition to my investigative duties, I am currently the Asset Forfeiture Coordinator and Organized Crime Drug Enforcement Task Force Coordinator for the Central California District. I also participate in community outreach and assist in firearms and enforcement training in our District.

The most important day of my career as a federal law enforcement officer was probably the first day, when I swore an oath to God to support and defend the Constitution of the United States. I have always taken that oath very seriously. With members of my family watching, I swore to the following words:

I, Joseph R. Banister, do solemnly swear, that I will support and defend the Constitution of the United States against all enemies foreign and domestic, that I will bear true faith and allegiance to the same, that I take this obligation freely without any mental reservation, or purpose of evasion, and that I will well and faithfully discharge the duties of the office on which I am about to enter, so help me God.

The above oath is very powerful. I have always relied on it to guide me in my responsibilities as a federal law enforcement officer. I have also been mindful of maintaining my ethics and moral standards as a public servant. The importance of these standards is summarized in a paragraph from the Introduction contained in Chapter 1 of the Internal Revenue Service Rules of Conduct (Document 7098 (7-86)):

Confidence in the Service and faith in its dependability and integrity are factors having a vital impact on our ability to carry out our purpose. We can maintain the public confidence only to the extent that every one of our contacts with the public reflects the highest ethical and moral standards.

Executive Order 11222 of May 8, 1965, the language of which is included in the Department of the Treasury, Minimum Standards of Conduct, at 31 CFR Part 0, Subpart A, Section 0.735-3, states:

Where government is based on the consent of the governed, every citizen is entitled to have complete confidence in the integrity of his government. Each individual officer, employee, or advisor of government must help to earn and must honor that trust by his own integrity and conduct in all official actions.

Further, throughout my career in public service, I have remained cognizant of the Internal Revenue Service *Mission Statement*:

The purpose of the IRS is to collect the *proper* amount of tax revenues at the least cost to the public, and in a manner that warrants the highest degree of public confidence in our integrity, efficiency and fairness. (Emphasis added)

. . . which was recently revised to state:

Provide America's taxpayers top quality service by *helping them understand* and meet their tax responsibilities and by applying the tax law with integrity and fairness to all. (Emphasis added)

The previous excerpts are but a small sample of the

principles promulgated by Department of the Treasury, the Internal Revenue Service, and the government in general. Adhering to the highest standards of honesty, integrity, morality, impartiality, ethics, trustworthiness, and loyalty to the United States of America are clearly a necessity for public servants working in a government which derives its authority from the consent of the governed.

In 1997, I was presented with an opportunity to determine whether or not I was really serious about abiding by those standards. I was presented with allegations relating to the very profession I had chosen and the very agency I was employed by, namely the public accounting/income tax profession and the Internal Revenue Service, respectively. Among the allegations presented to me was that (1) the federal income tax is voluntary and the filing of federal income tax returns is not required, that (2) the 16th Amendment to the U.S. Constitution was never ratified, and that (3) federal income taxes are not used to operate the Federal Government. Needless to say, these allegations were not only unbelievable but they were contrary to everything that I had been taught and contrary to everything I believed to be true. Notwithstanding the unbelievable nature of these allegations, they came from a source that I had found credible in the past. The credibility of this source was so strong that I felt more investigation was warranted.

I assumed from the beginning that I would have trouble convincing top officials in the IRS Criminal Investigation Division that government resources should be committed to investigating these allegations, serious though they were. This assumption is due to the ridicule that is commonly laid upon anyone who speaks of such matters. Most people espousing such beliefs about the federal income tax are usually dismissed as being crazy, a racist, a militia member, or a tax protester. I do not fit into any of those categories and neither does my source. Therefore, in order to both seek the truth and avoid ridicule, I made up my mind to investigate the allegations off-duty and at my own expense.

As I said previously, these allegations were contrary to everything I knew to be the truth. Therefore, I was prepared for the possibility that upon closer investigation, these allegations might prove to be just another scheme to distort the facts or the law, as the Internal Revenue Service has claimed in the past. I believed that my background in the areas of income tax law, income tax compliance, and income tax enforcement would enable me to separate fact from fiction. The results of my personal investigation were far from what I expected.

In short, based on my education, training, and experience, I believe that the allegation regarding the voluntary nature of the income tax does have merit and it is therefore immoral and illegal to fine, prosecute, or otherwise penalize those who do not volunteer. I also believe that, contrary to public perception, the income tax is not used to supply the Federal Government with needed operating revenue. I fully realize that my conclusions regarding these issues may have far-reaching consequences. However, based on the obligations and duties I described previously, I believe I must bring these matters to your attention.

I continue to have the utmost respect and admiration for those I have worked with not only in the IRS Criminal Investigation Division but all federal and state law enforcement officers and prosecutors. I have found these officials to be of the highest character and talent. I would like to continue to work with these officials but due to the nature of the allegations and evidence contained in my report, I am strongly considering resigning from the Service. Ultimately, my decision will hinge upon the Service's response to this letter. If the Internal Revenue Service will commit – in writing – to conduct its own point by point answer/analysis of the allegations and evidence set forth in my report, I will consider remaining in my position. If the Service declines to conduct its own analysis, or dismisses the evidence in this report without proper review, then I must tender my resignation. My oath to support and defend the Constitution of the United States was made to God and I can not serve two masters.

I have enclosed a copy of a report I prepared called *Investigating The Federal Income Tax: A Preliminary Report*, which summarizes the allegations and the evidence supporting them. I respectfully request that you simultaneously review this report and forward it to your superiors up to and including Commissioner Rossotti. I respectfully request that the Commissioner or his designee respond to the evidence in my report within 30 days. I am certain that IRS management will have questions and I will do my best to answer them. Please advise them that my email address at work is XXXXXXXXXXXX and my office telephone is XXXXXXXXXX. Written inquiries can be sent to Special Agent Joseph R. Banister, IRS Criminal Investigation Division, XXXXXXX, San Jose, California 95113.

Sincerely,

Joseph R. Banister
Special Agent
IRS Criminal Investigation Division

Well, Agent Banister simply wanted some answers. What he got was suspended! He was sent home and ordered to decide if he could continue to work as a special agent of the IRS. He decided that he could not. After receiving no response to his investigation and having his concerns go entirely ignored and being threatened with his job for raising legitimate concerns about the integrity of the Internal Revenue Service, Joe Banister resigned his position on February 25, 1999.

Then in typical IRS fashion, they went after Banister criminally. In November of 2004, Joe Banister was indicted on four felony counts. He prepared a very intelligent and truthful defense to these fabricated charges and was completely acquitted by a jury of his peers in June of 2006.

Joe Banister fought the beast and won. Many others have not been as fortunate. For his courage and integrity, Joe Banister is hereby inducted into the Hall of Honor.

* * *

The patriots honored in this chapter have demonstrated how we take America back. We get more of us standing together with our sheriffs and county commissioners, and we ride Dick Carver's bulldozer all the way to Washington, DC. Yes, there are a few needed repairs there, too! We must all follow their example and stand for true principles on behalf of the people.

Chapter 4

MY OPINION OR YOURS

Principles of freedom are not subject to the various opinions of the public, nor are they contingent upon the beliefs of politicians. Freedom was there from the beginning; we are born with it; it's innate. It really carries very little significance whether or not you like guns or if you think your neighbor should own one or fifty or none. Quite frankly, it is none of your business if your neighbor owns an Uzi or a Street Sweeper shotgun. Your neighbor is not subject or answerable to your opinions. My opinion, your opinion, or that of all the barbers on Main Street do not matter and have no bearing on my freedom or your personal choices. If your neighbor is not a criminal and has no intention of committing a crime whatsoever, then what he keeps in his closet by way of ammunition or firearms is none of your concern. Is it not wonderful that we live in a country where your freedom is not predicated on the opinion of your peers, neighbors, or government leaders? Your freedom is not mine to trifle with or alter in any manner unless you overstep your freedom to the point of reducing mine. When it comes to understanding the Constitution there is only one opinion that matters; that would be the opinion of those who wrote it. Discover their intent and you will discover the most amazing principles of happiness and self-determination ever imagined. You will discover the immutable principles of freedom that made us a nation, that made America the bastion of liberty and the strongest country in the history of the world.

Your opinion as to what sort of vehicle your neighbors might drive is just that: your opinion. And it is meaningless in the entire scheme of things. The people who wrote the Bill of Rights knew what they were doing and there was complete unanimity when it came to the right of the people to keep and bear arms. Their opinions mattered; their intent in formulating these protections was paramount. Vince Lombardi once said, "Winning isn't everything, it's the only thing." When it comes to America, freedom is everything and it **is** the *only* thing! It should not be altered or changed due to the personal likes or dislikes of you of your neighbors. Under our Constitution, freedom is not debatable and it is never up for a vote.

Freedom *is not served cafeteria style!* We do not have the prerogative to move through the line and pick and choose which freedom entrees we want and which ones we wish to ignore. "Oh yes, I'll have a little of that freedom of speech, and some of that delicious freedom of religion, and a double helping of that right to peaceably assemble. However, I'd like "Big Brother" regulations regarding the right to keep and bear arms. That right gives me indigestion; never liked guns much." Can you imagine such a country? Well, you don't need to. This is the America we live in – the middle of the road, "freedom in moderation" America – instead of the original "Live Free or Die" America the Founders fought for. (This is the state motto of New Hampshire and appears on all New Hampshire license plates.) Freedom can never be reduced to a pick-and-choose process. Approaching freedom with such an ignorant and arrogant attitude will produce one result and one result *only:* The cafeteria will close altogether, and all we will be left with is the soup line. We will be forced to live with the choices others will make for us. Sound familiar?

History has shown us the catastrophic results when we trust politicians with our personal safety. "Suffer not yourselves to be betrayed with a kiss." [10]

Guns, Drugs and Prohibition

Prohibition is another handcrafted political tool for tyranny. It is as common as taxes and just as de-

---

10 Patrick Henry, speech to the Virginia Convention, Richmond, Virginia, March 23, 1775

structive. Its exploitation creates abuse, corruption, and overcrowded prisons. Prohibition has been a huge failure, regardless of its supposed intention. Prohibition did not work in the 1920s to stop liquor consumption, it has not produced any success in diminishing the availability of street drugs today, and it will do nothing to reduce gun violence. Analysis of all three of these categories manifests significant historical evidence that laws of prohibition actually exacerbate the problem they were supposedly intended to resolve. Nevertheless, the prohibitionists will smell blood in the water of every highly-publicized incident and gather with an insatiable hunger for more laws, more taxes, more government, and more controls like ravenous sharks gobbling warm flesh. "Zero tolerance!" is their siren song, and all the while the loss of civil liberties worsens, taxes and man-power are wasted and fellow human beings are warehoused in the huge business of prisons. Which brings up another joke: We cannot even keep drugs out of our most secured locations imaginable; the prisons are full of them! Prohibition never has been an answer to social calamities. A police state cracking the whip over the heads of the people only breeds contempt and destroys trust and free will.

One hundred fifty years ago a backwoods lawyer sat as president of the United States and issued a pro-clamation about the dangers of prohibition. President Lincoln said, "Laws of prohibition go beyond the bounds of reason in that they attempt to control a man's appetite by legislation and make crimes out of things that are not crimes. A law of prohibition strikes a blow at the very principles upon which our government was founded." Lincoln's logic is essentially this: prohibition simply does not work. Whether it is aimed at booze, pot, or guns, it does not work!

If you examine all the efforts nationally to eradicate drugs and their disastrous effect on our society, what benefit can be ascribed to all this work and money? (Seventy billion dollars annually.) Well, drugs are more potent, more available, and more profitable. Forty years of the war on drugs and look at our amazing success! Now, even if there were some *magical* way to dissolve our nation's drug abuse and addictions, we would still have the greater scourge: tyranny and a dearth of constitutional obedience. Is there anything appealing about the attainment of drug-free tyranny? Similarly, the benefits of a gun-free society just do not seem to be too comforting, except to police and criminals.

The black market our government claims to be fighting was created as a direct result of our laws of prohibition. Making marijuana illegal increased its value by 500%. Would you like to decrease its value and the huge profits enjoyed by the cartels? Well then, a reversal of these laws would appear to be a logical alternative. But instead of applying logic, we will do more of what has previously failed, and of course, expect a different result!

Freedom has once again been the casualty of supposed good intentions, but it matters very little to the vapid politicians as long as the law perpetuates spending and garners votes. In the March 14, 1994, issue of TIME magazine, there appeared an article titled, "Who Should Keep The Keys?" The subtitle was, "The Federal Government wants the power to tap into every phone, fax, and computer transmission." Why? It's for our own good to be sure! They want to take care of us! They need this constitutionally forbidden power "to keep tabs on drug runners, terrorists, and spies." Now, don't you feel better, safer, and more secure? The government only wants unbridled power and authority to protect us! Is that not the same rationale they use for gun control? Their consistency is frighteningly magical.

Chapter 5

JUDGE JOHN M. ROLL

On January 8, 2011, Federal District Judge John Roll was gunned down by a maniacal and cowardly lunatic. Since this unspeakable and unimaginable tragedy, much has been said about who may have prompted its occurrence. Some of this rhetoric bordered on the absurd. I would much rather talk about the good people who had their lives snuffed out before their time and to pay tribute to who they were and what they stood for. Certainly, a beautiful little nine year old angel named Christina Green deserves to have her life displayed as an example to others to learn from and enjoy. I would like to say a few words on behalf of one of the victims, a man who changed my life and helped alter the course of American history: Judge John M. Roll. He was an honest man and a principled judge. He stood for what he believed was right despite the possible consequences.

I met Judge Roll back in 1994. In fact, it was in his courtroom. He was the judge who first heard my lawsuit against the Clinton Administration. Judge Roll had the courage to take a strong stand against the very entity that controlled his salary and career. He actually had the temerity to tell Congress and President Clinton that they exceeded their authority when they made the Brady Bill a law.

I was extremely nervous when I walked into Judge Roll's courtroom. A big crowd of supporters, reporters and cameramen had gathered outside the courthouse. Although I had been to court many times before as part of my duties as a police officer and sheriff, this was the first time it was in front of such a crowd and with such media attention, and in federal court no less. I remember looking at Judge Roll and relaxing somewhat; he had a kind face and was rather young, about my age. He had already sided with me in at least two pretrial motions that he had ruled on, both in my favor. The first one was the Federal Government's attempt to remove me from the case entirely by claiming I had no standing to sue them in the first place. They argued that only the county's Board of Supervisors could represent the county in such legal actions. Judge Roll said this was wrong because it was the sheriff being commandeered by the Federal Government, both officially and personally. Next, my lawyer asked for an injunction against the government from being able to arrest me for "failure to comply." (There was an actual provision in the Brady Bill that threatened to arrest the sheriffs if we failed to comply with this unfunded mandate from Congress.) Judge Roll seemed legitimately concerned about this bizarre threat throughout the entire lawsuit. Janet Reno herself wrote a memo to the Judge and assured him that the feds had no intention of arresting me and that the threat of arrest within the language of the Brady Bill was only intended for the gun shop owners, not the sheriffs. Judge Roll, as he announced his decision regarding the injunction, said that Janet Reno was not allowed to change the law "by fiat" nor interpret the law for Congress. "Mack's injunction is hereby granted," the judge said calmly and sternly.

Then as the hearing proceeded I was called to the stand. The butterflies returned big time. As the Justice Department's lawyer cross-examined me, she did something unusual; she actually began to address the judge while I was still sitting on the stand. She said, "Your honor, already in just the first four months of the implementation of the Brady background checks, we have denied over 250,000 felons from gaining access to handguns in this country." I was thinking to myself what a crock her numbers were and wondering why we had so many felons in America walking the streets and all trying to buy handguns in government checked gun shops. Suddenly, Judge Roll interrupted the attorney and rebuked her with, "Counselor, do not pretend in this courtroom that your statistical analysis somehow equates to constitutionality." I have to say that Roll's understanding of principles amazed me. He was so professional and knowledgeable. He took his job and the Constitution so seriously. He was truly an exemplary justice.

When Judge Roll issued his ruling on the Mack v. US case on June 28, 1994, he said two things that absolutely floored me. The first one was the order of the court which summarized his findings:

"The Court finds that in enacting [the Brady Bill] Congress exceeded its authority under Article 1, section 8 of the United States Constitution, thereby impermissibly encroaching upon the powers retained by the States pursuant to the Tenth Amendment. The Court further finds that the provision, in conjunction with the criminal sanctions its violation would engender, is unconstitutionally vague under the Fifth Amendment of the United States Constitution."

Judge Roll, of all the dozens of Judges who had heard this case from me and the other six sheriff plaintiffs, was the only one who ruled that the Brady Bill violated the Fifth Amendment as well as the Tenth. It was pursuant to Judge Roll's insight and sensitivity to the threat this "law" posed to us, the sheriffs, that this case made it all the way to the US Supreme Court.

When I read the other Judge Roll principle, it truly brought me to understand how astonishing this man really was. He said:

"Mack is thus forced to choose between keeping his oath or obeying the act, subjecting himself to possible sanctions."

To have a federal judge actually grasp the full extent of my personal motivation for filing this case was absolutely remarkable. He touched my soul with this comment and it is recorded in my books and memory forever. He was truly of the same mind as the Framers of the document whose tenets he so faithfully defended. Now, his work is a part of American history. His legacy is one of honesty, courage, heroism, and oath-keeping. He was a true defender of our nation's rule of law. Judge Roll left this world in typical Judge Roll fashion: He threw himself in front of the coward's bullets to save another potential victim and took a lethal wound to the heart as he did so.

This hero of a man changed my life and showed us all that the Constitution is still the supreme law of the land.

Chapter 6

ROSA PARKS

It was December 1, 1955 in Montgomery, Alabama. A seamstress was going home from work and got on the bus just as she always did early in the evening. Christmas music was coming from the local five and dime store. The lyrics of a Christmas carol could be heard faintly in the background, but there was no "good will toward men" in Montgomery this night. Why? Because Rosa Parks sat in the wrong seat! Don't you know that blacks had to get to the back of the bus? Sure, we were a nation conceived in liberty and dedicated to the proposition that all men were created equal. In fact, the United States Supreme Court had sanctioned the notion that we were all created equal with a doctrine known as "separate, but equal" which meant that the laws of segregation in America could continue as constitutional. What?

Well, let's finish the story. Mrs. Parks got on the bus and took a seat next to another black man, directly behind the section reserved for whites. At the next stop a white man got on the bus. The white man stood at the front of the bus for a moment and could not see an available seat. Noticing the passenger's predicament, the bus driver got up and announced that he needed the blacks to vacate the entire row of seats in which Rosa was sitting. The other passengers moved obediently to stand in the back of the bus, but Rosa did not. She remained defiantly in her seat.

Now rather perturbed, the bus driver approached Rosa and bent over to look her right in the eye. "Are you going to move?," he asked glaringly. Rosa stared right back at him. She swallowed and took a deep breath. Now shaking her head Rosa succinctly responded, "No." The bus driver was more than taken aback by her audacity. So, he warned Rosa that he would call the police and have her arrested. You see, this was not just a stupid tradition, it was actually a stupid law! But Rosa was ready for the consequences and informed the driver, "You may do that, sir."

So, the bus driver got off the bus, used a nearby payphone and called the Sheriff's Office. Two deputies responded to the scene of the crime and *arrested* an American citizen for failure to give her seat to a white man. She was handcuffed and hauled off to jail. At the jail she was booked, fingerprinted, photographed, and incarcerated. Later, bail was posted for her and Rosa went home to find her husband very concerned about her actions. He knew that Rosa could just have signed their death warrant. What Rosa did was worthy of retaliation and "purging" from local marauders. In America! Laws of hate and bigotry were being enforced by "peace officers" and sheriffs who swore an oath to defend and protect the constitutional rights of all people within their jurisdictions.

A constitutional officer or sheriff would have responded in somewhat of a different manner. Imagine it playing out like this instead:

* * *

The sheriff entered the bus, investigated the complaint a little further, then walked up to Rosa Parks and asked, "What seems to be the problem here ma'am?"
Rosa responded, "Why can't we just be left alone? Why does everyone have to push us around?"
The bus driver, disgusted, then said to the sheriff, "Will you listen to that?"
The sheriff then tactfully told the bus driver that he did not need his assistance and to continue on to the next stop. The driver complied, but more than just a little reluctantly.

The sheriff then sat down next to Mrs. Parks and said, "Mrs. Parks, what you did here this evening took a lot of courage and I'd like to shake your hand."

Rosa looked at him bewildered, almost thinking the sheriff might be trying to trick her. She shook his hand and felt his sincerity.

"Mrs. Parks, where do you get off the bus?"

"Two stops farther, on Elm Street."

"If you don't mind I'd like to escort you home. I want to make sure you get there safely. My deputy here will go with us. I want him to know where you live."

"Why do you want him to know where I live?"

"Because ma'am, he's going to be assigned to give your home extra patrol the next few days to be sure nobody gives you any trouble."

"That would be nice, thank you, Sheriff!"

The sheriff and deputy arrived with Rosa at her home and her husband panicked. The sheriff noticed Mr. Parks' concern at the sight of a couple of police officers accompanying his wife home, and held up his hand as if stopping traffic.

"It's okay Mr. Parks, there was a little trouble on the bus. Your wife refused to give her seat to a white man. Now listen, everything is going to be just fine. But can I ask you a personal question?"

"Sure, I guess so."

"Do you have a gun in the house?"

"Well, yes I do, a 12 gauge shotgun. Why?"

"There could be some trouble because of this bus incident with Rosa and even though my deputy here is going to be patrolling your home throughout the night and some other deputies doing likewise during the day shifts, we cannot be here every minute.

So keep that shotgun handy and should you need to defend yourself and your family, well, let your conscience be your guide. Your gun is loaded, isn't it?"

"It wouldn't do me any good if it wasn't, now would it, Sheriff?"

The sheriff nodded with a little chortle and bade the Parks goodnight.

* * *

That, my good friends, would have been a constitutional sheriff. Would he have been enforcing the law? Yes, but not the stupid one! He would have been keeping his oath, serving and protecting and not allowing societal norms to dictate how he did his job. This good sheriff would have been upholding the Constitution – the supreme law – and would have been putting the stupid state statute in the trash, right where it belonged! Good sheriffs and peace officers should be doing the same all across America today.

Let's take a closer look at our own history. Rosa Parks was not the only one to be punished for being in the way. Does May 4th, 1970 sound familiar? It was at Kent State University in Ohio. The Ohio National Guard came to campus to "keep the peace" during a student protest of the Vietnam War. The students were all *unarmed*. Nevertheless, soldiers fired 67 rounds at the students, killing four and wounding nine others. Some who were shot were merely passing by and were not participating in the protests whatsoever. They were just in the way. As a result of these murders no one went to jail; no one was even charged with a crime.

Randy Weaver knows what this feels like. His son and wife were shot and killed by federal snipers at his home at Ruby Ridge, Idaho in August of 1992. Was Weaver's wife shot in the head while holding a high-powered assault rifle, a bomb, or maybe a hand grenade launcher? No! She was holding her 11 month old baby, Elisheba. No one was charged; no one went to jail except Randy Weaver. He owned a shotgun with a barrel cut 1/8″ too short! Another gun control law protecting us all.

And who can forget the deaths by burning or bullets of 80 men, women, and children (including two women with unborn children) in the spring of 1993 in Waco, Texas? The federal snipers from Ruby Ridge got some more practice with live targets there. Of course, the FBI claimed no pyrotechnic devices were ever used or deployed in any manner at Waco and claimed that the compound was burned by its leader in a huge suicide pact by those who remained inside the church. Well, it turned out there *were* spent pyrotechnic devices used at Waco that were hidden in some FBI evidence locker. No one went to jail and no one was charged, except some of the Branch Davidians who survived the inferno. They got 40 years!

Let's all take a brief jaunt up in our helicopters and look down at these tragic catastrophes. There were no heroes at Kent State. There were none at Ruby Ridge and there certainly were none at Waco! Oh yes, there were many federal agents and officers with badges and men in uniform, but innocent and unarmed people died anyway. Somebody in uniform, somebody with a badge and a duty to protect should have stopped the shooting at Kent State. Somebody with a badge and common sense should have stopped the siege and subsequent killings at Ruby Ridge and somebody with a badge should have stopped the massacre at Waco, Texas!

Rosa Parks was a hero! She taught us all what we should do with *stupid* laws. However, we should have never heard of Rosa Parks, because someone in uniform, someone with a badge, should have prevented her arrest. Someone wearing a badge and uniform should have defended her right to life and liberty. And someone should do this today, for "Rosa Parks" the gun owner, all the "Rosa Parks" Americans who just want to be left alone.

Speaking of stupid laws, did you know that even farmers who sell raw milk are not free from harassment? Yes, we actually have the FDA and some states raiding farms and arresting farmers who do not pasteurize the milk they distribute. Believe it or not, there are actually quite a few people who prefer that the dairy products they consume be natural and organic, not burned. Dairy products have more nutritional value when they are not burned! When will government leave people alone and allow us to live our lives as we choose? Just for the sake of freedom, the first chance you get go buy some raw milk, or raw cheese, or ice cream from one of your local raw milk farmers. Most of the Amish deal in it and many others do also.

Chapter 7

Double take the Double Standard

New York City's murder, rape, robbery and aggravated assault rates rose in 2010 according to preliminary FBI data, with murders alone increasing by more
than 12 percent. But instead of concentrating on
crime in New York City, Mayor Bloomberg recently
spent $100,000 of the NYPD's budget to send former
police officers now working as private detectives to
Arizona with hidden cameras to show how easy it is
to buy guns at a gun show. They attended the
Crossroads of the West Gun Show in Phoenix. The
owner of this particular gun show is Bob Templeton,
who runs the business with his daughter in a very
honest and professional manner. Bob Templeton
and his family are friends of mine. Mayor
Bloomberg, you are no Bob Templeton!

This undercover stunt was a waste of money that

was intended to mislead Americans and it did nothing to reduce crime. Arizona officials had not been informed of the operation, which meant that any potential crimes uncovered by the New York City officers could not have been in accordance with local laws. There was no potential to enforce any violation of the law by the proper authorities. Bloomberg has no jurisdiction in Arizona, leaving us to conclude that there could have been no other motive here than a publicity stunt, intended to blame gun shows in Arizona for the increasing crime rate in New York City.

Instead of spending $100,000, Bloomberg could have learned what he was searching for in Phoenix for the price of a phone call or an internet search. Arizonans, like residents in 31 other states, can buy guns from private individuals without a criminal background check, just an Arizona driver's license to demonstrate residency. However, if they sell a gun to someone who they suspect will use it to commit a crime, they risk becoming liable for that crime.

John Feinblatt, a Bloomberg adviser, said, "The background check system failed in Arizona, it failed in Virginia and it fails in states around the country. If we don't fix it now, the question is not whether another massacre will occur, but when." Brilliant!

But background checks on the private sales of guns would not have stopped the Tucson, Arizona shooting. The killer, Jared Loughner, would have passed the background check at any gun store. He had never been convicted of a crime, never been adjudicated as being a danger to himself or others, and he had not been involuntarily committed for mental illness. Thus, he would have been able to get a gun in any state, **including New York**, where he had been a resident.

Background checks do not stop bad guys from getting guns. Instead, the Brady Act background checks for gun purchases, in place since 1994, are a problem for law-abiding citizens. Hardly ever do background checks deny guns to criminals. Over 99.9 percent of purchases initially flagged as being illegal under the law were later determined to be misidentified. Most of them were denied for minor traffic offenses or fishing license violations.

Contrary to public misdirection, very few criminals obtain their guns from gun shows. This was shown in an extensive survey conducted by the Bureau of Justice Statistics in 1997, with interviews of 18,000 state prison inmates. Only a trivial 0.7 percent indicated that they had obtained their guns at a gun show.

The overwhelming majority of guns that criminals obtain come either from "friends and family" (40 percent) or "on the street or from other illegal sources" (39 percent).

Mayor Bloomberg's little undercover ruse played

into the public's brainwashing of the magic of gun control, but as far as protecting his constituents, Bloomberg's blooper was a complete waste of time and money. (But what do politicians care about those sort of things?) Background checks, waiting periods, and registration will make us safer! Trust Bloomberg: he's rich; he knows! He is indeed one of our most renown Republican *polimagicians*.

The hypocrisy runs so rampant that it's nearly impossible to piece it all together. It certainly is impossible to reconcile. For instance, Rosie O'Donnell has been a self-appointed critic of gun owners for decades. Her infamous rantings aimed at Tom Selleck are her own personal demonstrations of freedom-hating and gun-grabbing madness. She has incessantly told Americans to not use or own guns. She promotes the magical malice of gun control – but only for the peasants. You didn't know? Yes, she has hired gun-toting bodyguards for years. But for those of us who cannot afford such high priced protectors, too bad! She has her protection but preaches to all others to avoid such for themselves! Ms. O'Donnell has made herself an easy *target* through her own transparent hypocrisy. But she clearly is not alone. Every anti-freedom, anti-Second Amendment politician in this country makes use of armed protection.

The "Gun-grabbing Hypocrite of the Year" award, however, goes to State Senator R. C. Soles, a Democrat from North Carolina. Senator Soles is a lawyer and the longest standing legislator in North Carolina. He has a negative view of gun ownership for the peasants, but as we learned recently, he keeps a gun in *his* home.

As an attorney, Senator Soles has had relationships with many of his clients and former clients that have been described as "weird" and "dubious." He has had numerous petty complaints and calls to the police ranging from disturbing the peace to assault. Putting this case into perspective may be the most daunting task of the decade, but here goes:

In August of 2009, two clients were pounding on the Senator's back door. The Senator was scared; he later said he thought they were breaking into his home, so he decided to get his *pistol*. He grabs his gun *that he does not believe in, does not call the police,* and instead shoots one of the possible intruders in the leg. The Senator claims the shooting was self-defense, but the investigation proves otherwise. The investigator stated that the people have the right to protect themselves, but he claimed what Soles did was "taking the law into his own hands."

Furthermore, the shooter was a lawyer who knows the law and he was also a Senator who made the laws, but did not support the law that he swore an oath to uphold known as the Second Amendment. The incident was thoroughly investigated and a grand jury handed down an indictment against the Senator for aggravated assault. Whew!

In the end, the senator takes a plea bargain and gets the felonies reduced to a simple misdemeanor and gets probation with a mere $1,000 fine. A $1,000 fine? Good grief, there are traffic violations that cost more than that! Was the shooting actually an act of self-defense or was it the overreaction of an elderly, corrupt public official? If you can sort through all this and come up with some reasonable conclusions to this convoluted mess, well then you ought to be a writer for the next CSI TV series. The only real conclusion is that this case is more politics, hypocrisy and irony from the usual source: another one of our political entertainers, the *polimagician* from North Carolina.

Chapter 8

Guns in America

There are over 300 million guns in the United States; about as many guns as there are people. Not only is gun control against the law here, but the feasibility of gun control while considering such staggering statistics makes even the thought of confiscation an exercise in futility or extreme absurdity. It is just not going to happen. However, that does not mean politicians will not attempt to do so. But what we do know is this: Where guns are most prevalent, crime is at its lowest and where gun control is most stringent, crime is at its highest. Therefore, laws against gun ownership in places such as Washington, DC, New York City, Chicago, and Detroit, have actually made gun violence and criminal activity worse in those areas.

Such laws prompted two recent landmark rulings from the Supreme Court. The first was that of Dick Heller, a DC special police officer authorized to carry a handgun while on duty at the Federal Judicial Center. He applied for a registration certificate for a handgun that he wished to keep at home, but the District refused. He thereafter filed a lawsuit in the Federal District Court for the District of Columbia seeking relief pursuant to the Second Amendment of the US Constitution. (The first federal court to hear this case ruled that the Second Amendment only protected the right of *Militias* or the *National Guard* and accordingly granted no relief to Mr. Heller. This is quite a bizarre stance for the court to take since the National Guard was formed in 1903, over 100 years after the creation of the Second Amendment.)

The appellate court disagreed with the outrageous and baseless decision of the lower court. Consequently, the US Supreme Court granted certiori (agreed to hear the case)[11] and yes, in a 5-4 decision, the Court held that the Second Amendment protects an individual right to possess a firearm unconnected with service in the military, and to use that firearm for traditionally lawful purposes, such as self-defense within the home. The Court based its holding on the text of the Second Amendment, as well as applicable language in *state constitution*s adopted soon after the Second Amendment. Justice Antonin Scalia delivered the opinion of the Court. Justices John Paul Stevens and Stephen Breyer filed dissenting opinions, each joined by the other as well as Justices David Souter and Ruth Bader Ginsburg. Amazing

11 District of Columbia v. Heller (No. 07-290)

isn't it? The four liberals on the Court sided with the government's effort to promote gun control. Justice Stevens also argued that the Second Amendment only protects the rights of individuals to bear arms as part of a well-regulated state militia, not for any other purposes, even if they are lawful. (You see what happens when we fail to learn from history?!)

The second case was McDonald v. Chicago[12]. Otis McDonald – a black man from Chicago – believes he has the right to keep and bear arms. Where would he get such an idea? He certainly didn't get it from Jesse Jackson! McDonald was exasperated with the gun control laws of Chicago and wished to be free and independent of the whims of local politicians. McDonald decided to sue on the grounds that the City of Chicago had to obey the Second Amendment. Chicago maintained that the Second Amendment and the recent Heller ruling only applied to the Federal Government. Does anyone find it the least bit strange how every official in the city of Chicago – each and every one of the local lawmakers – who supported gun control regulations, who swore an oath to obey the Constitution for the United States of America, could somehow justify nullifying said oath and declare that the Constitution does not apply to them? Why take an oath of allegiance to this foundational American ideal and then argue – in Federal court no less – how it has no applicability to you or your office?

---

12 McDonald v. Chicago, 130 S.Ct. 3020 (2010)

So, McDonald took his legal plight for liberty to the courts and lost the first two rounds. But the Supreme Court of the United States reversed the lower courts and ruled that the Second Amendment is a law that States and the political subdivisions thereof must comply with. As surprising as it may be, the Supreme Court ruled that the Second Amendment must be adhered to by the States due to the technicalities of the Fourteenth Amendment. The requirements of due process and the equal protection clause of the Fourteenth Amendment must be obeyed. Yes, and so should the right of the people to keep and bear arms, but the Court took a backdoor approach to that principle by way of the Fourteenth Amendment. Another very pertinent aspect of the Fourteenth Amendment reads, "No State shall make or enforce any law which shall abridge the privileges or immunities of citizens of the United States..." It just so happens that one of the abuses we are immune from is *gun control*.

McDonald won his case. Have you seen the NAACP lauding his victory? Why? Because the political agenda of the "Obamaites" simply does not allow for such, even if it is for a fellow American who just happens to be black! Should not freedom be for all people, of all races and all colors? We discriminate against certain liberties that seemingly don't fit into the vogue issues of the day. Could such a process ever equate to "...liberty and justice for all?"

Chapter 9

FREE THEM, BUT DON'T ARM THEM!

The history of the United States is saturated and deeply scarred by "laws" of prejudice and hate resulting in widespread civil rights violations and even mass murder. Before the Emancipation Proclamation *and* the Civil War, the "law" allowed whites to own blacks. Even after slaves were "freed" they were forced to live under laws of extreme racial prejudice. By "law" blacks were prohibited from eating in the same restaurants as whites, from living in the same neighborhoods, from using the same hospitals, or even from using the same water fountains. These "laws" were all enforced by our nation's police and sheriffs, regardless of their morality or constitutionality. (All laws have to be enforced, right? It does not matter how horrible or abusive, if the politicians pass it the police will enforce it!)

Furthermore, even as freemen of America blacks were denied the right to own guns. When angry mobs of hooded marauders came to burn homes, perform whippings or lynchings, "free" black citizens were forced to stand by helplessly and watch as loved ones were brutalized and murdered. The best escape was often found in servile obedience and submission. Yet, gun control laws then came with the same labels and propaganda as they do today: "It's for your own good", or "It's best for society."

Another page of American history involved an exodus west by some in pursuit of land, wealth, and better lives. As these trailblazers moved into the new territory, they found other cultures and civilizations inhabiting their own promised lands. Native Americans were slaughtered for being in the way. These first Americans were later left defenseless through government agreements which required Indians to give up their weapons. Millions died.

Another disgrace in America was the incarceration of Japanese Americans during World War II. In Gestapo fashion, the US Government rounded up all Japanese in the land of the free (especially those living along the west coast) and put them in concentration camps until the end of the war! There were no warrants. No crimes had been alleged and not one trial took place. Nevertheless, concentration camps were filled, the Constitution was forsaken and the compromise completed "for the good of the nation." Does any of this sound familiar? The Patriot Act is based on the exact same premise: Compromise freedom for security!

Let us not pretend that DC receives all the culpability with such politically correct criminal behavior; there's more than plenty to spread around. Let's travel 225 miles north to the Big Apple. It was November 29, 2008, in a midtown nightclub on Lexington Avenue. Plaxico Burress – an all-star football player for the New York Giants – was at the Latin Quarter nightclub having a few drinks with a friend and teammate, linebacker Antonio Pierce. Burress felt the need to be armed. Why should he carry a gun? What does a celebrity football player have to fear these days? What difference does it make? Should any American have to explain why he exercises his right to keep and bear arms? Some kings believe so. The peasants should all have to bow and kiss the royal ring, ask for regal permits, and follow the whimsical rules of those in power.

Nevertheless, Mr. Burress had a gun, in a nightclub, and within NYC. Did he try to shoot someone? Did he attempt to rob the establishment? Did he threaten anything "subversive" like joining the NRA or worse yet, a local *militia* group? No, this successful all-star had no such intentions and certainly intended to commit not a single crime. So why is Plaxico Burress in prison? Because he was in a city and state that do not respect the Bill of Rights, and accordingly, his liberty was stripped.

In the wee hours of the morning in the Latin Quarter nightclub, for some unknown reason, Burress grabbed his pistol and it accidentally discharged. The music was loud and with most patrons pounding out moves on the dance floor, the blast from the gun brought little attention from anyone. However, Pierce heard it and saw that the bullet actually hit Burress in the leg. Pierce rendered first aid and scolded Burress for bringing the gun to the club. Burress was so afraid of the police that he refused an ambulance. Pierce likewise tried to cover up the shooting to save his friend from New York's finest. However, after Pierce did everything he could to get Burress home as surreptitiously as possible, Burress's wife intervened and took him to the hospital. From there, the police were notified and the New York "justice" system started its inquisition.

Burress was looking at 3½ years mandatory for felony possession of a firearm. He then became part of the plea bargain extortion program, also known as the contemporary torture chamber. "If you take our plea bargain offer we will only destroy your career and family and rob you of your freedom for two years instead of 3½. You are so lucky we are making this offer to you. Normally we would just toss similar lawless dirt-bags in the hole and throw away the key. We are showing you some mercy." This may not be the exact words used by the police and the District Attorney's office, but it is quite similar and it is the exact result. "Take the deal or you will be sorry, it will be worse for you and your family if you don't take it!" This is their offer of mercy!

So Burress was made "an offer he couldn't refuse" and appeared in court to make it official. He got permission from the king to hug his little boy and his wife just before he was hauled off to prison. Good job, New York and Mayor Bloomberg, you are really cleaning up the city! We are all feeling so much safer knowing that such criminals like Plaxico Burress are no longer on the streets. We can all head to Broadway plays now with the assurance that we'll be much safer and protected. *It is magic!*

What benefit did Plaxico's prison sentence provide the city of New York? Having a man in his prime robbed of his job and possibly his career, unable to provide for his family, torn away from his son and wife, his precious liberty stripped from him like a slave at a Sunday afternoon auction! If Burress had done such a stupid thing in a nightclub in Montana or Wyoming the police would have laughed at him for being so clumsy. Yes, what he did was stupid, *not criminal!* Hells bells, if we threw people in prison for being stupid 90% of our nation's leaders would be there. (The other 10% would have taken all their millions and run away to Costa Rica!)

Any reasonable person would have to wonder where in the world was the NAACP. Did they not attempt to intervene on behalf of the Burress family? Does not the NAACP realize how many blacks are incarcerated (enslaved) by such ridiculous and racist laws? Where was Jesse Jackson? Was he not planning a boycott and a protest with Al Sharpton? What happened to Plaxico Burress should never happen to any American! This is an absolute outrage and a pathetic miscarriage of justice. If we followed our Constitution – the supreme law of America – Plaxico Burress would be home with his family and preparing for his next touchdown! Instead, Burress was forced to endure the chains and slavery of gun control laws. His enslavement occurred with tacit approval from those who should have prevented it. "But the Constitution protects us from our own best intentions."[13]

---

13 It is a pleasure to report that during the final preparation for printing of this book, Plaxico Buress was released from prison and has returned to football. The tragedy and hypocrisy surrounding his time in prison remains a lesson to us all.

Chapter 10

FREEDOM BUTS

In the Mack/Printz ruling, the Supreme Court put into historical context the power of the states, noting that it was actually the 13 original States that formed the Federal Government. During this foundational process Justice Scalia said that the States "surrendered many" of their powers to the new Federal Government, but "they retained a residuary and inviolable sovereignty." This is one area where Scalia erred in this landmark decision. The States did not *surrender* anything when they created the central government; they *delegated* some powers and assigned the National Government **a few** (not many) *discreet and enumerated* duties. If an employer (the States) delegates or assigns an employee a few tasks or jobs (such as border security), and then the employee does not do his work or performs it an unsatisfactory manner, then would it not be reasonable and proper for the boss to terminate the assignment, delegate the work to someone else, or to simply take the job back and do it himself? Oh no, not in government! Instead, Obama sues Arizona, claiming *supremacy!* There are two teensy weensy problems with this. First, the States retained "a residuary and inviolable sovereignty" and second, the supremacy clause of the Constitution does not grant omnipotence to the national authority. The supremacy clause states:

"This Constitution, and the laws of the United States which shall be made in pursuance thereof; and all Treaties which made, or which shall be made, under the authority of the United States, shall be the supreme law of the land..."

So how does the Federal Government obtain supremacy? By making laws and treaties "in pursuance of" the United States Constitution. Therefore, there could be no supremacy shared by the Federal Government, because they have not done anything in pursuance of the Constitution in over five decades. The feds diminish their own supremacy on a daily basis as a direct result of their own constitutional disobedience. Trampling on the Constitution creates no supremacy and certainly obligates no one to go along with such criminality.

Furthermore, if the States retained an inviolable sovereignty and are therefore *NOT* subject to Federal direction, why do they not run their own affairs, control their own lands, parks, education, air, rivers, forests, or *health care?* If the States are indeed free and independent as stated within the Declaration of Independence, then why do we all bow and kiss the ring of the EPA, OSHA, TSA, DHS, DEA, IRS, and all the other hundreds of bureaucracies in Washington? They are not our bosses! Bureaucrats have no authority to run our States! Virginia should be run by Virginians, Florida should be run by Floridians, Arizona should be run by Arizonans, Texas should be run by Texans (I think you get the point). If the president of the United States cannot tell the States what to do, and if Congress has no authority to tell the States what to do; then how in the world did the EPA obtain such power?

We are free, *but...*

Chapter 11

WOMEN AND GUNS

When a paroled ex-convict forced his way into a posh Florida home on March 12, 2011, he had no idea what awaited him: A 25-year-old beauty queen with a pink .38-caliber handgun. Pink? That's right, real women pack *pink* heat! Meghan Brown – who reigned as the 2009 Miss Tierra Verde – shot and killed 42-year-old Albert Franklin Hill during a home invasion this past March at the 2,732 square foot house she shares with her fiancé in Tierra Verde, Florida.

Robert Panthaber – a 42-year-old arborist and Brown's fiancé – said he believes the two of them were targeted because of their wealth. He claimed a pizza delivery man and possible accomplice staked out the home for three months before Hill attempted to burglarize it.

"We live in a very prominent area and my fiancee

wears a $60,000 engagement ring," he said. "The pizza man knew we had money because sometimes we needed change for a $100 bill when he came to deliver pizza."

Hill had a criminal record stretching back nearly three decades including arrests for burglary, battery, drug possession and grand theft. He reportedly served a 13-year prison term in 1987 and was released in September after serving a fourth term behind bars.

Hill forced his way into the home at around 3 a.m. after Brown responded to a knock at the front door, according to the police report. The ex-convict demanded money and then a physical struggle ensued. The suspect grabbed the 110-pound Brown around her nose and mouth and dragged her to an upstairs bedroom.

Panthaber said in an interview that he was quickly awakened by the altercation and ran to Brown's aid. "I attacked him and took a severe beating to the head," he told Fox News. "But I got him off of her long enough for her to scramble to the room where she keeps her pink .38 special."

Police say Brown snatched her gun from a nearby bedroom and shot the suspect several times, hitting him in the chest, groin, thigh and back. Hill was pronounced dead at the scene. (Her grouping would have given her a less than average score at the gun range, but she got the job done. The bad guy lost, the petite beauty queen won!)

Detectives with the Pinellas County Sheriffs' robbery & homicide unit are still investigating the crime, but believe the motive was robbery, according to local press reports. They say they haven't yet determined the relationship, if any, Hill had with the couple.

Panthaber says he and his fiancée are lucky to be alive. He had just purchased the pink handgun for Brown the previous Christmas. (Could you really receive a more worthwhile present for Christmas than one that saves your life?) Panthaber also said that the two had gone to target practice together. "She was not a good shot at the range," he quipped. Proof once again that you don't have to be an expert marksman to take care of yourself in a shooting situation.

The summary of cases and incidents that demonstrate the effectiveness of women defending themselves with guns is irrefutable; a woman is better off with a gun, as are we all! National statistics prove that when women use a gun to fend off a would-be attacker, the result is complete safety and success for the potential victim 87% of the time.[14] No other method of self-defense even comes close to that of using a gun! An armed woman will come out unscathed 87% of the time.

---

14 Richard Mack, "From My Cold Dead Fingers", 2000

Let me present you with two very likely scenarios. First, the society WITH gun rights:

The local Women's Club is having their monthly meeting at the county library. There are about 50 women in attendance. Suddenly in the middle of the meeting, some scuzzy looking freak walks into the meeting room and screams at the women to get down on their hands and knees. Startled and bewildered, the women all look at each other, shrug their shoulders, and reach into their purses. Half of them pull out snub-nosed revolvers and point each one at the dirt-bag who had just interrupted their meeting. One woman proudly announces that last month's meeting was a training session on handgun self-defense. The armed intruder stares in disbelief and turns white with fear at the sight of a dozen guns pointed at his head. He decides to drop his gun. The ladies surround him and keep him prone on the floor until the police arrive. A white haired 80-year-old woman puts her gun back into her purse and proclaims happily, "I am so glad I did not miss last month's firearms class!"

Or, the society WITHOUT gun rights:

The perpetrator storms into the Women's Club meeting, points his gun at these innocent and defenseless ladies, then methodically begins to execute them one by one. Choose which scenario you prefer. There is no middle ground here, there is no negotiation, there is no alternative. You are either armed or you are a target. Which society do you want to live in? Which one do your "leaders" want to force you to live in? (Note that in either scenario, the perp has a gun. We all know why: It's because *lawbreakers, by definition, break the law!*)

Should we not all do our part to keep our neighborhoods safe? Refusing to arm yourself makes you dependent upon those who do.

This is America! This is the "right to keep and bear arms" and this is the benefit of self-defense. The happy ending above is not an illusion. The "magic" and collateral benefit of armed defense is that more often than not, you do not need to shoot the suspect or "bad guy." Simply displaying your gun or brandishing your weapon (or the sound of a shotgun jacking a shell into the chamber) is all it takes to stop the assault, attack, robbery, or rape. Professor John Lott authored a book, "More Guns, Less Crime" and in it documents that guns are used hundreds of thousands of times annually in America for self-defense, and reiterates the undeniable truth in these incidents: A vast majority of them end peacefully without a shot ever being fired. Show the pistol or rifle to the assailant, and he will go running home like the coward he is. We all know that criminals prefer unarmed victims. This fact is absolute; it is undeniable! What criminal would NOT prefer an unarmed victim? So, the solution is that each of us should...? Come on now, you know the answer. Go ahead, say it. Finish the sentence. That's right; each of us should be armed. It is NOT magic! It's the most obvious trick ever. Any true political magician would shudder at the thought of you, the unsuspecting public, finding out the way it really works. Carry a gun, stop crime. No increased taxes. No new laws. No federal mandates. No government entity gains any authority. You can see why the *polimagicians* hate the idea.

Chapter 12

GUN CONTROL IS AGAINST THE LAW!

Propaganda schemes advocating government's authority to regulate Second Amendment rights are lies taught in many of our schools today. They cannot afford to teach children what the Framers said about the right of the people to keep and bear arms and why this principle was such an integral part of the movement for liberty. If we taught that principle in our schools students might actually believe it, and the agenda to create more socialism and gun control might be impeded. And what would happen if we taught these principles as expressed by our Framers to our nation's police? Heaven forbid that our peace officers would actually discover that gun control in America *is against the law!*

No cop is obliged to enforce an unconstitutional law.

The fact that other government officials violate the Constitution puts no obligation on anyone else to go along with such treachery. The brainwashing of political correctness would have us believe that if the government does something wrong the victimized citizen must file a lawsuit and seek "justice" through the court system. But how well does that work out? Let me see if we all have this straight: If the government violates the law – or does not keep within the rules – then John Q. Citizen, who objects to such lawlessness, must spend all his life savings and the next 3 to 10 years fighting an injustice that all government officers swore an oath to protect the citizen from in the first place. The citizen loses either way. It is more practical and honorable for "public servants" to exemplify some semblance of integrity, keep their word, and interpose themselves on behalf of the people. It is more reasonable to assume that no sheriff or peace officer would willingly participate in jeopardizing the liberty of an American citizen.

When functioning correctly, our form of government does one vital thing: It protects the little guy from overreaching and tyrannical rule. Is this not what America was supposed to be about from the beginning? There is a long list of abuses our form of government was specifically designed to prevent. It can be found in a little-read document called the Declaration of Independence, where the oppressions we suffered under King George III are given in detail. I won't quote it all here but I encourage you to read it on your own and see if you find any similarities with where we are now. If not, then perhaps you'll get a nice peek at where we'll be soon enough.

Careful examination of America's origin leads us to conclude that the Framers of our Constitution had no intention of creating the freest country in world history only to have this entire system of individual rights based on the whims of judges who are appointed for life to their omnipotent positions. They never intended that the ultimate declarations of what personal freedom would or would not be would all rest with a nine member oligarchy in Washington, DC, otherwise known as the US Supreme Court. Furthermore, our system of constitutional checks and balances was never to be contingent upon a costly and unreachable court system. There simply is not sufficient time nor money for victimized citizens to seek justice in this manner. The States, counties, and cities must understand their jobs and fulfill their obligations to the people; then court cases regarding government abuse will be practically unheard of. Do local governments know what state sovereignty is? Are we all waiting for the president to appoint the States' Rights Czar? Who is supposed to enforce state sovereignty or the Tenth Amendment? Does anyone imagine that this duty is the Federal Government's? Who decides how far the Federal Government can go? At the present moment, *they do!* James Madison said, "We can safely rely on State Legislatures to erect barriers against the encroachments of the national authority." Don't look now, but that means the *states* are charged with the constitutional duty of keeping the feds where they belong. "Hence a double security arises to the rights of the people. The different governments will control each other."[15]

Consider how this often-repeated yet seldom understood section of the Declaration of Independence would read if the current thinking was applied to it:

"We hold these Truths to be self-evident, that all Men are created equal..." (Only if the courts say so,) "That they are endowed by their Creator with certain unalienable Rights..." (Only if the courts say so,) "That among these are Life, Liberty, and the pursuit of Happiness – " (Only if the courts say so.) "That to secure these Rights, Governments are instituted among Men..."

This is the only place in all our country's foundational documents where we see the true intended purpose of our form of government: **To secure these rights!** Which rights? Life, liberty, and the pursuit of happiness (ownership of property). Therefore, if any form of government at any level is not securing life, liberty and property, then that government is unnecessary, unconstitutional, and meaningless if not downright harmful. Such government becomes "destructive of these ends" and thus, has no place in

---

15 Justice Scalia, Mack/Printz v. Unites States (95-1478), 521 U.S. 898 (1997)

America. We needn't honor, obey, or respect such lawlessness. We must, as the Founding Fathers said, "Throw off such government." Freedom is still the answer and is the only thing worthwhile as a result of having any government. Today however, programs, policies, entitlements, and politics have replaced that liberty endowed by our Creator.

Chapter 13

THE FOUNDERS

It has been rationalized by contemporary criminals that the Constitution no longer applies to us today, or that because it is a "living document" it is subject to the norms and standards of our supposedly more sophisticated modern America. One such proponent, Richard Stengel, the Managing Editor of TIME magazine, said the Founders could not have known how to forge laws and rules applicable to the grandeur of our cities or the capacity of our weaponry. Therefore, we have the right to ignore what we will; we now know what's best. Of course, Stengel wrote this yellow journalistic trash in the Fourth of July issue where one might think TIME would pay tribute to our freedom protecting Constitution. Not hardly! Stengel actually listed numerous examples of contemporary advances which the Framers could not have known about, which therefore renders our antiquated Constitution useless in today's world! TIME and Stengel tell us this because the "Framers did not know about DNA, sexting, computers, miniskirts, or Lady Gaga." Man oh man, you can't argue with brilliance like that now can you!? This is what we are told; this is today's propaganda; this is today's political brainwashing!

Has America really changed since its birth? Is there anything the Framers wrote that is no longer applicable? Of course, who needs all that freedom nonsense today? The Bill of Rights can't apply to us today; we have computers and Lady Gaga! Yes, Stengel specifically mentioned *Lady Gaga!*

Let's look back at some events from the exceptional life of one of the foremost Founding Fathers, Thomas Jefferson. As you're reading, ask yourself these questions: Was he qualified? What kind of value system did he have? Does anything he learned still apply today?

Age 5: Began studying under his cousin's tutor.
Age 9: Studied Latin, Greek and French.
Age 14: Studied classical literature and additional languages.
Age 16: Entered the College of William and Mary.
Age 19: Studied Law for 5 years starting under George Wythe.
Age 23: Started his own law practice.
Age 25: Was elected to the Virginia House of Burgesses.
Age 31: Wrote the widely-circulated "Summary View of the Rights of British America" and

retired from his law practice.

Age 32: Was a Delegate to the Second Continental Congress.

Age 33: Wrote the Declaration of Independence.

Age 33: Took three years to revise Virginia's legal code and wrote a public education bill and a statute for religious freedom.

Age 36: Was elected the second governor of Virginia, succeeding Patrick Henry.

Age 40: Served in Congress for two years.

Age 41: Was the American minister to France and negotiated commercial treaties with European nations along with Ben Franklin and John Adams.

Age 46: Served as the first secretary of state under George Washington.

Age 53: Served as vice president and was elected president of the American Philosophical Society.

Age 55: Drafted the Kentucky Resolutions and became the active head of the Republican Party.

Age 57: Was elected the third president of the United States.

Age 60: Obtained the Louisiana Purchase, doubling the nation's size.

Age 61: Was elected to a second term as president of the United States.

Age 65: Retired to Monticello.

Age 80: Helped President Monroe shape the Monroe Doctrine.

Age 81: Almost single-handedly created the

University of Virginia and served as it's first president.

Age 83: Died on the 50th anniversary of the signing of the Declaration of Independence along with John Adams.

Thomas Jefferson understood what was needed for a successful government because he had studied the previous failed attempts at government. He understood actual history, the nature of God, His laws and the nature of man. That happens to be way more than what most understand today. Jefferson really knew his stuff, and *the truths he understood and intentionally embedded into our founding documents still apply today!*

John F. Kennedy held a dinner in the White House for a group of the brightest minds in the nation at that time. He stated, "This is perhaps the assembly of the most intelligence ever to gather at one time in the White House with the exception of when Thomas Jefferson dined alone."

Here is a selection of essential Jefferson quotes. I think you'll agree these are TIMEless in their applicability:

"When we get piled upon one another in large cities, as in Europe, we shall become as corrupt as Europe."

"The democracy will cease to exist when you take

away from those who are willing to work and give to those who would not."

"It is incumbent on every generation to pay its own debts as it goes. A principle which if acted on would save one-half the wars of the world."

"I predict future happiness for Americans if they can prevent the government from wasting the labors of the people under the pretense of taking care of them."

"My reading of history convinces me that most bad government results from too much government."

"No free man shall ever be debarred the use of arms."

"The strongest reason for the people to retain the right to keep and bear arms is, as a last resort, to protect themselves against tyranny in government."

"To compel a man to subsidize with his taxes the propagation of ideas which he disbelieves and abhors is sinful and tyrannical."

* * *

How far have we fallen from these "Jeffersonian" ideals? Compared to the republic Jefferson visualized for us, are we even recognizable as a nation? We would be far better off to listen to the TIMEless words of Jefferson than to Richard Stengel and TIME magazine with their politics of the moment.

The petrifying aspect of all the rationalization in today's political structure is that it contains no parameters or limitations. Government can do whatever it wants as long as "it's a good idea" or it somehow benefits the nation. Respect the rules? No, the president does not have to. The United States Congress does not have to. Governors do not have to. State reps and senators do not have to. But, if they make *new rules* then we, the peasants, have to obey those rules. Of course, if we don't then we go to jail, yet nothing happens to them for violating the original rules, the supreme rules of the land. Have we totally lost our minds?

"But the Constitution protects us from our own best intentions. It divides power among sovereigns and among branches of government precisely so that we may resist the temptation to concentrate power in one location as an expedient solution to the crisis of the day."[16] Wow! "The Constitution protects us" from "good intentions" and "the crisis of the day." What has been the mantra of the Obama administration? "Never let a good crisis go to waste!" (Even if you have to create one.)

The Constitution either means what it says or it means nothing at all. If governments can do

---

16 Justice Scalia, Mack/Printz v. Unites States (95-1478), 521 U.S. 898 (1997)

whatever they like and mandate gun control/registration or healthcare or water turnoffs to the Napa Valley in California then they can do anything! Only out of control narcissistic politicians could find excuses to circumvent our Constitution to promote their own selfish agendas and anti-American programs. If you wish to change the Constitution, there is a lawful process granted within the Constitution itself by which such changes may be achieved. There have been a total of 27 amendments to the Constitution since its inception and even some amendments removed. Change it if you will, but until then, every public official has sworn to uphold and defend it, as mandated within the Constitution itself! For my part – whatever anguish it may cost – I am willing to accept the risks associated with freedom. I also concur with the intent of our Founders to bind politicians down with the chains of the Constitution. In the 60s and 70s the slogan in America was "give peace a chance." Sure let's try it! But maybe we could achieve that lofty goal by giving the Constitution a chance. (We have not used it in decades.)

The Constitution is not magic. It is only as strong as the hands of those who have promised to preserve it. But let's make no mistake here. Ambiguity simply is not an option. Freedom is for people of all races, of all colors, of all religions; it is for all Americans. The Constitution was designed specifically to protect equal opportunity and personal liberty. Can we really afford to embrace ideology that moves us away from those ideals?

The propaganda to destroy our right to keep and bear arms today has been devastatingly successful; so much so that even our textbooks promote it. Authors no longer strive to teach our foundational principles and instead re-write our history to support their fictional claims. You see, the Second Amendment states clearly that "the right of the people to keep and bear arms shall not be infringed." Of course, this is the latter half of this most vital protection of freedom. The first part, "A well regulated militia, being necessary to the security of a free state," is what many of our school propagandists love to distort. They will actually claim – straight-faced no less – that the reference to the "militia" is talking about the army or National Guard.

So let us put this farce into proper perspective. The teachers, professors, media, politicians, etc., who attempt to sell (brainwash) this notion, would have each of us believe that whilst the Framers of our Constitution were so arduously pounding out a new experiment of freedom based on the power of the people and not the power of government, working through their personal differences and the heat and humidity of a Philadelphia summer, they took a timeout from this labor, completely changed gears and decided to make a law to protect the right of our soldiers to keep and bear arms! There is not one historical reference from any of the signers of the Constitution which corroborates this modern day hocus-pocus, that soldiers were somehow in need of having their rights to possess arms protected or guaranteed. Nor is there any mention by James Madison in his copious notes of the goings on of the Constitutional Convention, that any of the Founders ever expressed their fears or concerns about soldiers of the Continental Army would somehow lose their right of keeping or bearing muskets. They certainly had difficulty with funding and purchasing necessary supplies to adequately fight the Revolutionary War, but the soldiers still had guns! Plain and simply, the Bill of Rights was written to protect the people from government, not to protect the rights of the government itself!

There are two other huge problems with this little illusion. First, the Founders would have had to have been clairvoyant, as the National Guard did not exist until about 100 years later. Second, the "militia," (yes, the 'M' word) is not referring to a branch of the armed forces. In Article 1, Section 8 of the Constitution, the Framers wrote that Congress had the power to,"raise and support armies, but no appropriation of money to that use shall be for a longer term than two years." (So the Founders were against a long standing permanent army.) Yet just two lines later the same section says that Congress can call forth the "militia" to execute the laws of the nation..." So is there a difference between the army and the militia? Clearly there is. Richard Henry Lee said, "The militia, when properly formed, is comprised of the people themselves and consists of all men capable of bearing arms."[17] George Mason issued a parallel statement to that of Lee, "I ask sir, what is the militia? It is the whole people.... To disarm the people is the best and most effectual way to enslave them."[18] Oh those founder guys, they were always saying such radical things!

So, there was no contradiction within the Second Amendment and teachers or politicians attempting to make such claims are either ignorant or lying. The militia is now and always has been, just as the Constitution begins: We the People! The militia in 1776 was the minutemen; it was us! The Founders of America knew what they were talking about, and liberty is just as valid and necessary today as it was in 1776. There was no more magic back then than there is now.

---

17 Richard Henry Lee, "Letters from the Federal Farmer to the Republic", 1788
18 George Mason, in *Debates in Virginia Convention on Ratification of the Constitution*, Elliot, Vol. 3, June 16, 1788

Chapter 14

NOTHING NEW

Essential to the idea of property rights is the freedom to defend one's property, person and family. Without the right to defend what you own, the right of ownership is meaningless and hollow. It is essential to note here that the Second Amendment was not devised as a protection for the possession of sporting weapons, nor was it originally intended as a provision for individual self-defense. Fortunately, weapons used for gathering meat and warding off criminals are also effective for discouraging governmental tyranny. The Founding Fathers carried fresh recollections of the repugnant nature of King George III's despotic rule, and they designed the simplest of the ten amendments comprising the Bill of Rights to forever prevent a recurrence.

The fight between good and evil is as old as history itself. Philosophies of socialism, communism, Marxism, and other forms of aggressive, dictatorial government are nothing new. The greatest civilizations throughout recorded history have crumbled from within, destroyed by epidemic corruption, excessive taxation, and moral and social decay. Oppression and tyranny have always come from government, and desires for liberty and freedom have always originated from the masses. As has been said many times, those who refuse to learn from the pages of history are doomed to repeat it. It was governmental tyranny and oppression which drove the Founders toward the making of America, a new nation based on God's law and "dedicated to the proposition that all men are created equal."[19]

During the previous two centuries of successful republican government in America there has occurred a gradual evolution toward the philosophies of Marxist socialism—the same philosophies responsible for enslaving and subjugating millions in the past. Americans are hearing the knock of tyranny at their doors, and the strongholds of liberty are giving way. The words of a 20th century world leader reflect the trends of the time: "This year will go down in history. . . For the first time, a civilized nation has full gun registration! Our streets will be safer, our police more efficient, and the world will follow our lead into the future." Does this statement sound familiar? Reviews of nightly newscasts or video coverage on C-SPAN might suggest Charles Schumer, Diane Feinstein, Nancy Pelosi, Mayor Bloomberg or

---

19 Abraham Lincoln, The Gettysburg Address, Gettysburg, PA, Nov 19, 1863

Bill Clinton as the author of this "civilized" view on gun control. While its source has been disputed by some experts, others have given credit for this particular quotation to Adolf Hitler. Regardless, Hitler was unquestionably renowned for his devotion to gun registration and was an absolute gun control fanatic. Why would contemporary leaders attempt in any way to be like him or support philosophies similar to his?

> *"If every Jewish and anti-Nazi family in Germany had owned a Mauser rifle and twenty rounds of ammunition AND THE WILL TO USE IT Adolf Hitler would be a little-known footnote to the history of the Weimar Republic."*
>
> ~ **Aaron Zelman, JPFO**

Gun and other arms control is nothing new. Before guns existed governments attempted to confiscate swords, bows and arrows, spears, axes and knives. Edicts of this nature invariably led to mass murders, subjugations, slavery, and acts of genocide. Many attempts by governments to disarm, register or confiscate guns have been etched indelibly into our histories. And yet, not one specific incident of gun control, gun registration or any confiscation of weapons can be credited with saving lives, protecting citizens, decreasing violence, creating peace or securing principles of liberty.

Wake up, America! Has history taught us nothing?

In the relatively brief span of its existence, the United States of America has become recognized as the greatest country in the world. The reason? STRONG FEDERAL CONTROL! (Sorry... did anybody lose their lunch on that last line right there?) Let's try that again. The reason? **Freedom! FREEDOM!** The exceptionalism of America lies simply in personal liberty, defined by a guarantee that our government will leave us alone to live our lives as we see fit, not infringing on the rights of others to do the same. The blueprint for freedom has been our inspired Constitution, designed to protect God-given rights. The vision and knowledge of the Founders should serve as timeless lessons for continued success of the American Experiment. In 1787 Richard Henry Lee said, "To preserve liberty, it is essential that the whole body of the people always possess arms..."[20] Why then, would Schumer, Feinstein, Pelosi, Bloomberg, and the Clintons – along with many other politicians, mayors, commissioners, police officials and organized anti-gun groups – support the disarming of America, an effective death sentence imposed on the tenets of liberty? Such action in 1776 would have been considered treasonous. In contemporary times, cries of treason have given way to socialistic demands for mainstream "political correctness." Other Founding Fathers defined and defended the eternal principles of liberty. Patrick Henry, while trying to motivate his fellow countrymen to action in 1775, spoke of

---

20 Richard Henry Lee, The Pennsylvania Gazette, Feb. 20, 1788.

limitations on freedom: "They tell us, sir, that we are weak; unable to cope with so formidable an adversary. But when shall we be stronger? Will it be the next week, or the next year? Will it be when we are totally disarmed, and when a British guard shall be stationed in every house?"[21] Does this not sound like a description of President Clinton's 1994 crime bill, which called for banning weapons of defense and assigning as many as 100,000 additional police officers into private neighborhoods? This is nothing new and it certainly has no magic.

Thomas Jefferson quoted in his writings, "Laws that forbid the carrying of arms serve rather to encourage than to prevent homicides, for an unarmed man may be attacked with greater confidence than an armed man. Laws that forbid the carrying of arms. . . disarm only those who are neither inclined nor determined to commit crimes. Such laws make things worse for the assaulted and better for the assailants."[22]

The Second Amendment did not give men the right to keep and bear arms; self-protection is an unalienable right with which we were endowed by our Cre-

---

21 Patrick Henry, Speech at the Second Virginia Convention at St. John's Church in Richmond, Virginia, 23 March 1775

22 This is not something Jefferson wrote himself, but it is clearly something he believed very strongly as he had much to say on the subject. This quote is a modern English translation of a passage he included in his "Legal Commonplace Book." The passage is from Cesare Beccaria's Essay on Crimes and Punishments, originally written in Italian.

125

ator. The Second Amendment is a limitation to government power and a direct order for government to obey. Federal employees and public servants have a sworn duty to obey the Bill of Rights just as a soldier has a sworn obligation to respect the orders of his general. Imagine the chaos resulting from a soldier summarily refusing to obey an officer's command until he obtains an interpretation from the Supreme Court! We, the people of the Republic of the United States of America, are the generals in charge of securing compliance with constitutional orders as established by the Founding Fathers. Insubordination, government criminality, treason and usurpation of power cannot be tolerated. To allow these actions is to undermine the US Constitution. Furthermore, to undermine the Constitution is to threaten liberty and the very existence of America. Yet magical attempts to do so are *nothing new!*

Chapter 15
GREEN MAGIC: THE FEDERAL RESERVE

Article 1, Section 8 of the Constitution states, "The Congress shall have power...To coin money, regulate the value thereof, and of foreign coin, and fix the standards of weights and measures." This is one of the few enumerated powers specifically granted to the Federal Government, because it is one of the *very* few responsibilities that are better handled at the national level. This power ensures that all states have currency of the same value and promotes free and fair trade between them.

On December 23, 1913, Congress passed the Federal Reserve Act. It was signed into law by President Woodrow Wilson, and this was a defining moment in his presidency; one he later denounced as a huge mistake. Regrettably, that was about the only time President Wilson was right about anything.

The Federal Reserve Act has definitely been an illusion; it was pure *green magic*. The law was a result of the United States Congress relinquishing and abdicating their Constitutional duties to a private group of banksters.[23] This is power! And even more startling, right now all this power has been vested in one man, Federal Reserve chairman Ben Bernanke, and to foreign banks. For many years it was Alan Green-

> *"If the American people ever allow the banks to control the issuance of their currency, first by inflation, and then by deflation, the banks and corporations that will grow up around them will deprive the people of all property, until their children wake up homeless on the continent their fathers conquered ... I sincerely believe that the banking institutions having the issuing power of money are more dangerous to liberty than standing armies."*
>
> **~ Thomas Jefferson**
>
> **(It would seem that President Jefferson did not buy the bankers' magic!)**

span, appointed to this position by both Democrats and Republicans alike. These Federal Reserve Chairmen have been delegated power and authority that Congress was never authorized to give. The Chairman of the Federal Reserve – which is no more federal than Federal Express is – has the regal power to dictate the value of the American dollar, to dictate

---

23 http://www.urbandictionary.com/define.php?term=bankster

what interest rates will be and to report back to the banks who run and own the Federal Reserve.

Article 1, Section 8 details what Congress can do, what powers they have and overall, what their specific role is in our constitutional republic. Not at any time has there ever existed, nor is such ever mentioned in the Constitution, that Congress can delegate these enumerated powers to a private organization. For example, Article 1, Section 8 also states that Congress has the power to establish post offices and post roads. Could they reasonably and constitutionally turn such power over to the Boy Scouts of America? Furthermore, Article 1, Section 8 allows Congress to promote the progress of science and useful arts. Does this then somehow grant Congress the prerogative to summarily delegate this responsibility to the Mormon Tabernacle Choir? It is unquestionable that both the Boy Scouts and the Mormon Tabernacle Choir are very capable and worthy organizations, however, they possess no governmental or constitutional authorization to do anything except work on merit badges or sing at inaugurations. Likewise, Congress has no authority to delegate the power to regulate the value of our monetary system to private banks, Greenspan, Bernanke, or the man in the moon! It is *their* assignment and theirs only!

Furthermore, the Constitution directs that "No State shall emit bills of credit or make anything but gold and silver coin a tender in payment of debts." So, how is it that the States have to use gold and silver and the Federal Reserve can use paper "money?" How did that happen? The answer is both simplistic and criminal; Congress does not believe that they must adhere to the Constitution in the slightest. They do not understand "Congress shall make no law..." or "...the right of the people to keep and bear arms shall not be infringed" or "The right of the people to be secure in their persons, houses, and effects..." or "Excessive bail shall not be required, nor excessive fines imposed..."

Yes, the Federal Reserve is *green magic.* It takes gold and silver and transforms them capriciously into greenbacks, a fiat currency! A currency that is no longer backed by gold or silver. Most Americans buy this entire process as standard and routine. The Federal Reserve creates money out of thin air and simultaneously creates inflation. To watch the value of the dollar decrease annually (or now, daily) is what each American is forced to live with. Thank goodness for that cost of living increase each year!

Since the Federal Reserve took over our country's monetary system in 1913, the dollar has lost 95% of its value. Even more staggering is the fact that the Federal Reserve has never, that's right, *never* been audited! Now let's make certain we have this right; Americans are subject to random audits by the Internal Revenue Service, which results in fines and penalties and prison sentences. We are subject to a ruthless and Gestapo-like bureaucracy that has literally destroyed the lives of countless Americans. Yet, the Federal Reserve will not answer to any audits or oversight whatsoever!

President Ronald Reagan described our tax structure as the following: "Our federal tax system is, in short, utterly impossible, utterly unjust and completely counterproductive, it reeks with injustice and is fundamentally un-American..."[24] Why do we allow this perpetual plague to destroy our country and the lives of our neighbors?

"Fiat money is printed on demand and without limits. The over production of such money destroyed the economy of Germany after WWI. The Fed is completely controlled by foreign bankers who are profiting by America's destruction."[25]

Corruption and the DC syndicate continue as we search for solutions to the economic mess our politicians have allowed and created. But isn't it handy that this entire disaster can be resolved if we just get out there and vote for another Democrat or Republican! Ah, the *magic* of it all!

---

24 President Ronald Reagan, May 1983, Williamsburg, VA.
25 Congressman and Presidential Candidate Ron Paul.

Chapter 16

Can We Win?

American history has taught us that the brave patriots who stood against the British empire risked all for independence. They resorted to armed conflict and violence. Winning such a war against the most powerful and prolific military in the world surely seemed more than impossible. John Quincy Adams was asked if America could ever hope for victory against such an indomitable foe. Adams' reply was simply six words, "Duty is ours, results are God's."

When the first Americans were confronted with Britain's tyranny and proposed gun control laws, they responded accordingly. These patriotic Colonists refused to disarm! They would not give up their muskets and knew the disastrous consequences of doing so. Honor and liberty required their resistance. "Resistance to tyranny is obedience to God!" they exclaimed. So it was at Lexington Concord on the morning of April 19, 1775. This was the first "shot heard round the world," the official commencement of the Revolutionary War. It was the Colonists' response to British aggression and their attempt to confiscate or destroy a local arsenal. It was a gun control scheme the colonists would not tolerate! They fought a war to stop such abuse! Now we embrace such controls as a routine part of American politics!

Captain Parker was in command of the Lexington company. Word of approaching Redcoat platoons had already arrived. Now the sound of the British marchers could be heard through the Massachusetts' morning mist. The British Captain, riding a white stallion in front of his troops, yelled an order to the American Minutemen: "Lay down your arms you damned rebels, or you are all dead men!" These brave patriots refused. "Fire!" came the next order from the British Captain. Some Americans were killed and some retreated. A few crawled away wounded, only to die in the arms of their wives. They would not disarm! Our country's origin was based on a refusal to disarm! But now, in "modern" times our "leaders" would have us give up our weapons, saying that doing so will make us safer! "They who would give up essential liberty to purchase a little temporary safety, deserve neither liberty nor safety."[26]

Patrick Henry delivered his famous "Give Me Liberty, Or Give Me Death" speech in the Old North

---

26 Memoirs of the life and writings of Benjamin Franklin, 1818

Church on March 23, 1775, just a few weeks prior to the Lexington Concord battle. Henry was full of wrath and indignation when he stood to give this timeless and most stirring oration; he had just witnessed a preacher being flogged to death for preaching the gospel contrary to the British government's laws. Henry spoke with the power of God and asked why those listening would not get more involved in the fight against England. "Why stand we here idle?" Henry asked. "The battle, sir, is not to the strong alone; it is to the vigilant, the active, the brave. There is no retreat, but in submission and slavery!"[27]

George Washington had gained a widespread reputation for being the consummate soldier and leader. Even his enemies respected his ability and strength. Washington was elected to lead the Continental Army against Britain in the Revolutionary War. Without his powerful leadership, the war would have been lost in a matter of months. He saw the real potential of the effort and did not let the lack of supplies, money, support, or loyalty from fellow Americans deter his commitment. He loved America and liberty. The first two years of the war brought nothing but failure, discouragement, desertion, and staggering losses and casualties. Washington's vision and determination for freedom was not swayed, nor was it weakened.

---

27 Patrick Henry, Speech at the Second Virginia Convention at St. John's Church in Richmond, Virginia, 23 March 1775

On December 8, 1776, Washington moved across the Delaware River by ferry into Pennsylvania. Washington had the presence of mind to take with him all the boats within 50 miles. Thus, the Redcoats were incapable of following them anytime soon. The American army, *the entire army*, had dwindled to a mere 5,000 soldiers, most of whom were sick, exhausted, or starving, and nearly all of them were lacking adequate supplies or clothing. In fact, one of Washington's captains had written in his journal, "some of the men were naked, in every sense of the word." General Washington had made a similar entry in a letter, "You might have tracked the army from White Marsh to Valley Forge by the blood of their feet." Some soldiers had taken their remaining clothes (rags) and wrapped them around their feet to stop the bleeding from the impact of the ice and snow.

Now, stationed at Valley Forge, the Continental Army was making every attempt to regroup, acquire some much needed food and supplies, and get some medical assistance and rest for the infirm. Washington went so far as to have his wife transported to Valley Forge to aid in sewing clothes for the men. It was an astonishing process of teamwork and dedication; all did what they could for the "Holy Cause of Liberty."

However, Washington was never one to rest on his laurels. He knew his men needed to rest, but he also knew there was still a war for independence raging.

So, when you are tired, beaten, cornered with your back against the wall, starving, and hopelessly outnumbered, what should you do? Well, perhaps only the courage and strength of General Washington could have conceived this, but he decided to attack. That's right, attack!

Knowing that the Hessians (German soldiers hired out to Britain) made a great deal of Christmas, and knowing that these German soldiers occupied Trenton and would more than likely be drinking heavily to celebrate Christmas Eve, Washington decided to go back across the Delaware River and launch a most daring surprise attack in Trenton. A horrible blizzard was setting in and was making their march into Trenton all that more difficult, yet easier to conceal. Washington was moved to tears as he watched many of his still half-naked men march to glory while leaving tracks of their own blood. Regardless, he heard not one complaint.

Whispered commands from one soldier to another to remain absolutely silent through the entire march were passed down the chain of command. Escape routes were blocked by Continentals and the remaining soldiers were now in place. The American army descended with the wind at its back, which forced the snow into the faces of the enemy as they attempted resistance. Alexander Hamilton was the American artillery captain and his platoon fired their cannons at point blank range. In less than two hours Trenton was sacked. It was the best Christmas of General Washington's life. His men captured over a thousand Hessians, forty horses, hundreds of muskets, ammunition, and now enjoyed a Christmas celebration consisting of food, clothes and boots! It was miraculous! A beaten and poorly equipped army, motivated and led by this true hero and patriot, followed him to an impossible victory. Leadership and vision can conquer all obstacles and then maybe, just maybe, create miracles. Nevertheless, miracles never happen unless *we are moving*, working, and sacrificing. "Those who expect to reap the blessings of freedom must, like men, undergo the fatigue of supporting it."[28]

As Patrick Henry concluded his fiery and awe-inspiring speech in the Old North Church, he undoubtedly caught the attention of all those within earshot with the words, "Is life so dear or peace so sweet as to be purchased at the price of chains and slavery? Forbid it Almighty God! I know not what course others may take, but as for me, give me liberty or give me death!"[29]

Now, Henry's words ring both inspirational and hollow; perhaps meaningful back then, but utterly lacking in applicability to our sophisticated society today, aren't they? We are too advanced for such principles. We no longer need to put liberty before politics. Gun control is for our own good, as are all

---

28 Thomas Paine
29 Patrick Henry, Speech at the Second Virginia Convention at St. John's Church in Richmond, Virginia, 23 March 1775

other governmental programs and entitlements and debt and bureaucracy. What else do we need? Say a few magic words (to muddle your mind); a flick of the wrist (to take your guns) a wave of the magic wand of politics, and... *Ta-Da! Your freedom disappears!*

Conclusion

Is America Unsinkable?

This is the last chapter in the book. By now each of us should be able to answer the three questions asked at the beginning, on the *About This Book* page:

- Does gun control reduce crime and thereby make us safer?
- Does gun control pose any risks to our safety or security?
- Is gun control lawful and constitutional?

This might be a good time to look back and solidify our answers. We need to be sure enough not just to convince ourselves, but to help others around us see past the illusions as well.

President Clinton said during a state of the union address (in front of the entire country), "The era of big government is over." No one believed it then and nobody believes it now. The illusionists will not stop the lies and their lovely and well-paid assistants – the mainstream media – will not expose them for the two-bit magicians they really are.

Obama has used his "crisis of the day" fear-mongering every step of the way during his presidency. The "bailouts" were laced with threats of immediate doom and gloom if we did not continue to spend more than we had and borrow more to pay off previous loans. He warned if we did not do this and do it now, our economy would collapse! These same ridiculous scare tactics were used to pass Obamacare and all the other absurd tax-and-spend and borrow-and-spend DC disaster bills.

Those who risk their lives for our country by serving in the military are paid barely enough to live on, and then if they survive 20 years they receive a measly 50% of their salary for a retirement. Yet, the crooks in Congress bestow upon themselves huge salaries and retirements that would never be seen in the private sector. How is it that these "protectors and leaders" who assure us annually that they really care about the people, bestow upon themselves better benefits than they do on veterans? Right now Congress has the lowest approval rating in our nation's history: a mere 10%. Yet, how is it that we will still re-elect most of these inept *polimagicians?*

The catastrophe we are now facing in America is due to our failure to adhere to the principles our nation was founded upon. We should well know by now that the "The price of freedom is eternal vigilance"[30] but we have failed miserably in that regard. We have trusted our politicians and quite frankly, that has been a mistake of monumental proportions!

Our present predicament is analogous to the horrific and dreadful sinking of the Titanic. All on board this doomed ship slept comfortably with the assurance from arrogant leaders that all was well; the Titanic was unsinkable. This line from the illusionists of the day was a great way to get people on board and make headlines, but the very people making this magic knew the ship was made of iron and that it most certainly could sink! As the Titanic steamed across the North Atlantic and struck a mammoth iceberg, a gash 200 feet long was ripped into the ship's right side. Two hours later the "unsinkable" ship would be nearly two miles under water.

The initial impact and listing of the ship sent a wave of panic through the passengers as all scrambled for answers and solutions. The captain ordered women and children first into the insufficient lifeboats while the ship's band moved from playing upbeat ragtime to "Nearer My God To Thee," and fifteen hundred people died after falling into the calm, freezing ocean.

---

30 Often attributed to Jefferson, no original source for this has been found in his writings. The earliest established source for similar remarks are those of John Philpot Curran in a speech upon the Right of Election (1790), published in *Speeches on the late very interesting State trials* (1808)

The primary difference today is that yes, our country's ship is sinking, but our illusionists still attempt to convince us to stay the course. "Don't worry," they say, "we're going through some rough waters, but if we keep doing more of what we've been doing, we'll make it." It's as though the passengers of the Titanic had stayed in the great hall captivated by a magic show rather than filling the lifeboats.

Yes, we have bought into one of the greatest illusions of all, that America is unsinkable, regardless of who is steering the ship. Who do you vote for? It doesn't really matter. *America is unsinkable!* Just vote for whoever promises to give you the most stuff. The Constitution? Who needs it? *America is unsinkable!* The law is whatever suits your current purposes. We sit here arrogantly gorging ourselves in the dining hall on our unsinkable ship in self-indulgent decadence. We are rich, powerful and beautifully dressed and awaiting the evening show.

Then suddenly a lowly cabin-boy comes running into the hall. "Hey, everybody!" he cries out. "We're about to hit an iceberg! I saw it through a break in the fog!" None of us believe him. We stay in our seats; the opening music is playing. The boy goes back out to the deck and gets other passengers who also saw the iceberg. Soon there are hundreds of them forcing their way into the dining hall, yelling and shouting, "STOP! TURN AROUND! WE'RE HEADED FOR DESTRUCTION!" But the people seated in the dining hall are mesmerized by the magic show. Finally the desperate passengers realize what's going on and rush the stage, pulling back the magician's cloak and curtains to reveal his tricks, and suddenly what had been so captivating only a moment before is now obvious and infuriating. Not only did the magician intentionally distract the audience, he was aware of the iceberg all the time and had a private craft waiting to take him to safety after he had stolen everyone's valuables in the panic!

This is where we are, America. And what we need is not one lonely, scared voice in the corner; not even groups of people organizing protests across the country. We need an entire nation of people who finally see the iceberg ahead and stand firm in what they know to be right, wherever they are. It is time to turn this ship around, city by city, county by county, state by state. As I have made clear in my other books and presentations, local law enforcement (especially sheriffs) are key in this struggle but all of us have important roles to play, whether we hold public office or any other position of responsibility in our own communities, in our own homes or our own lives.

We must go back, not forward. If we return to those basic, fundamental principles of Creator-endowed rights and self-government, and hold firmly to the lifeboat of freedom, we will save ourselves and our country. But freedom only works if we keep making the choices that keep us free. The crew of the Titanic were free to charter any course they liked, until they hit that iceberg. After that, their choices became severely limited.

Yes, hold to your guns and bibles and get busy. Why do people make such a big deal about gun control? Because gun control is one of those 'iceberg' issues. We're free to do whatever we want with our guns, but *once we choose to give that freedom up there will be no getting it back.* We will be truly defenseless, not only against physical attack, but – and perhaps more importantly – against those who would attack other freedoms we hold even more dear. We will have sunk the ship.

If the right to keep and bear arms is denied, a quick glance through the Bill of Rights will tell you what will most likely be the next to go.

Professional Biography

Sheriff Richard Mack is an author, consultant, Tea Party activist, motivational speaker, constitutional scholar, teacher, and professional lawman. He has written five books and has been a consultant to lawyers and citizens battling cases of police abuse and other governmental misconduct. He has spoken at over 120 Tea Party rallies from Honolulu to Bangor, Maine. He has taught high school government, police academy classes, and currently trains sheriffs in the practical application of the Constitution as well as holding other classes and seminars nationwide. He is a law enforcement veteran of nearly 20 years.

Mack started his police career in 1977 in Provo, Utah as a parking enforcement cadet while working his way through college. In 1979 he became a full-time patrol officer. Soon he was promoted to corporal, front desk sergeant, communications supervisor, and detective. He also served as a patrol supervisor and school resource officer. His most traumatic experience while working for the Provo Police Department was a one year assignment as an undercover narcotics officer.

In 1988 Mack moved from Utah back to his home town in southeast Arizona to run for sheriff of Graham County. He was elected that year and re-elected in 1992. In 1994 he was the first sheriff in the United States to file a lawsuit against the Clinton administration to stop the unconstitutionality of the Brady Bill. Six other sheriffs from across the nation eventually joined the lawsuit. Sheriff Mack from Arizona and Sheriff Printz from Montana appeared together at the US Supreme Court in December of 1996. Then on June 27, 1997, the US Supreme Court agreed with these two small-town sheriffs and in fact, ruled the Brady Bill to be unconstitutional. The Mack/Printz case was a landmark decision on the issue of States' Rights and local autonomy.

While serving as Graham County Sheriff, Mack supervised an office of 30 full-time employees and approximately 65 volunteers. He also supervised the county jail, coordinated Search and Rescue, handled a budget of $1.8 million, taught DARE, and developed and enforced departmental policies and procedures.

Sheriff Mack's books:
- **From My Cold Dead Fingers** – Why America Needs Guns
- **Government, God and Freedom**
- **The Proper Role of Law Enforcement**
- **The County Sheriff: America's Last Hope** (also available as an audio book)
- **The Naked Spy** (A novel)

Mack has appeared on Good Morning America, MSNBC, CNN, Nightline, Crossfire, CBS Morning News, Court TV, FOX News' Freedom Watch, UNIVISION, BBC, Russia Today, Australian Broadcast Corp., Showtime's The American Candidate and over 500 radio shows nationwide.

He was named Elected Official of the Year by the AZ/NM Coalition of Counties, received the Firearms Industry of America CICERO Award, The National Sovereignty Council's Samuel Adams Leadership Award, and is the only person in history to receive the top Police honors from the NRA, Gun Owners of America, and the Second Amendment Foundation.

To contact Richard Mack, order books or schedule him for an upcoming event, please visit his web site:

www.sheriffmack.com